UNMASKED

The Courage to Be You

Scripture taken from the New King James Version®. Copyright © 1982
by Thomas Nelson, Inc. Used by permission. All rights reserved.

Published in collaboration with
Season Press and Fortitude Graphic Design and Printing
Cover and book design by Sean Hollins
Edited by Sonya Bernard-Hollins

For information regarding this book, bulk discounts or speaking
engagements please contact Morris Brooks at:
info@mobrooks1.com or visit: mobrooks1.com

Brooks, Morris, 19xx-
Unmasked/ Morris Brooks- Non-fiction
p.cm
1. Spirituality 2. Christian Living 3. Self Esteem 4. Peer Pressure

ISBN-10: 0986317322
ISBN-13: 978-0-9863173-2-3

Printed in the United States of America

SECOND EDITION
10 9 8 7 6 5 4 3 2

Dedication

I would like to dedicate this book to my late grandparents, Deacon Robert Lee Edwards and Audrey Edwards. My salvation is the fruit of your prayers and firm walk in Christ.

To Dr. Addis Moore and the youth of Mt. Zion Baptist Church in Kalamazoo, Michigan for your faith, encouragement and accountability.

Last, but not least, to my family, especially my mother, Paulette Brooks. You have taught me so much through your unconditional love. I love you!

Contents

FOREWORD

Unmasked is a refreshing and revealing way to see life with Christ. Minister Morris Brooks has allowed God to shape his life in a way so that his negative experiences can now be a blessing to others. He proves through his book that Romans 8:28 is certainly true, all things really do work together for good to those who love the Lord and are called according to His purpose.

In a time when so many people—especially young people, are struggling with their identities, trying to be someone else and are living unfulfilled lives, *Unmasked* gives hope and help.

Through his testimony, Min. Brooks is able to break through the barriers of low self-esteem, peer pressure, and loss of identity. He shows very powerfully and unapologetically that the Word of God and a relationship with Christ is the answer. He has taken off his mask, found his purpose, and now is able to lead others to do the same. As you read this book, it is my prayer that you are inspired, as I have become, and that you find hope, help, and healing.

Dr. Addis Moore,
Mt. Zion Baptist Church, Pastor

Dear Reader,

God will often ask us to do some things that may go against our society's norms. To be a Christian—especially a young Christian takes courage. However, your desire to please others will have to change into pleasing the One and only, God. It takes courage to live by scripture and to lead others to Christ. It takes courage to say no to popular things that may lead to sin. It takes courage to go against the cultural norms of the world for the sake of Christ. To live as a Christian is to live a life of courage.

That is why God encouraged Joshua, *to be strong and very courageous* (Joshua 1:7). God knew that times would get hard for Joshua. He knew that Joshua would have to obey Him when it was not popular, in order to lead others to where He promised they would go. Paul also encouraged Timothy through the Holy Spirit saying, *For God has not given you the spirit of fear, but of power and of love and of a sound mind* (1 Timothy 1:7). God wants us to have enough courage to let go of our sin and trust Him.

There are many professing Christians who attend church every Sunday only to leave to repeat the same sin habits they did before they walked through the church doors. There are many who cry to the Lord in conviction only to return to pick up the same struggles the next day. What about the person who has given up on church, but claim they still walk with Jesus? Have you encountered anyone like this? I know I have…because I have been that person.

It is not that Christians do not want to change, but for some reason we continue to revert to the same old behavior of the world. Young Christians (spiritually new youth) are being attacked by the world on every level. To just show up to church on Sunday will not do us any good without getting to know God on Monday, Tuesday, Wednesday, Thursday, Friday and Saturday! Although, simply going to church does not save us, believing in the Son of God, Jesus

Christ, will. This book will challenge you to be who God said you are in Christ every day and every place.

Some Christians who say Jesus is Lord, may not be the same ones doing His will (Luke 6:46). Why? Could it be, that we do not know who God is so therefore we do not reverence Him? Could it be we are scared of what others may think if we live for Christ and turn away from our sin? Is there so much temptation in the world that it is impossible for a young person to live as a Christian? Is the church not what you think it should be so you refuse to attend? Or, are we just simply not saved?

Think about why it seems so hard to live courageously for Christ. Be honest. If you do not love God, believe in God or desire God, tell Him. He can handle it. At the same time, ask for His help and take some steps toward Him. *Draw near to God and He will draw near to you. Cleanse your hands you sinners; and purify your hearts, you double-minded* (James 4:8).

If you are struggling with living for Christ and getting to know Him through the scriptures, then this is the book for you. If the Bible seems too intimidating to study, this book is for you. If you are afraid of what others think about you as you live out your faith, this book is for you.

Let us therefore come boldly to the throne of grace, that we may obtain mercy and find grace to help in time of need (Hebrews 4:16). We can come to God for help because He understands what we are going through. The purpose of this book is simply to build your relationship with Jesus Christ who is our Lord and Savior. It is meant to help build healthy study/prayer habits and live unmasked as a Young Courageous Christian. We cannot know God, if we do not know His Word.

I have hidden the word in my heart that I may not sin against You (Psalm 119:11). It is critical to remember the attributes of God and His Word so we may not sin against Him. The Word of God serves as protection against sin, but we may not have the Bible with us every time we are tempted. When some teenagers, young adults and new Christians attend Sunday school and are asked to do what God says, many don't know *who* He is or *why* they should obey Him. We need to know who He is in our daily lives to be able to worship, pray, respect, praise, love and obey God.

God is inexhaustible, which means we cannot know too much about Him. As Christians we will be spending eternity getting to know Him. When you complete this book, my prayer is you will be able to dive into the Word of God without doubting where to start or fear what others may think of your commitment to Christ.

This book will help you build a solid foundation upon the Word of God. It will help you hide the Word in your heart by memorizing scriptures and following its instructions to help protect you in the face of temptation, suffering and trials. So, get ready to be challenged, pushed out of your comfort zone and stretched!

Morris "Mo" Brooks,
Your Fellow Young Courageous Christian

Pre-Test
Who is God?
Why is it important to know Him?

It is so important to know the attributes of God. This is a great opportunity to see how much you know. Please do not be discouraged if you miss some of these answers. If needed, use the Word Pool below for assistance.

Example: God is the _____, therefore He created all moral and ethical laws. **Answer: Lawgiver**

God is _____ because He never has made a mistake, wrong decision or committed a sin.

God is _____ because He is like no other. He is set apart from everything and everyone.

God is _____ because He has unlimited power.

God is _____ because He is everywhere at the same time.

God is _____ because He knows all things (past, present and future; nothing is hidden from Him).

God is _____ because He will always and forever keep His promises! God is loyal and He cannot lie.

God is the _____ because all things are made by Him.

God is the _____ because He is the One who holds all things in place e.g. the earth rotation, planets orbit, and water separated from the land.

God is _____ because He is fair and all of His decisions are righteous.

God is _____ because He gives sinners time to repent.

God is _____ because He blesses sinners when they do not deserve it.

God is _____ for He sent His son to die for the sins of the entire world so that they may be saved.

God is _____ because He will punish and judge all sin.

God is _____ because He despises the worship of other things/people/idols.

God is _____ because He can do no wrong.

God is _____ because no one created Him. He has always existed. He is the beginning and the end.

Word Pool:

* Merciful * Righteous * Perfect * Jealous * Creator

* All-Powerful * Sustainer * Holy * Eternal (Self-Existing)

* All-Knowing *Loving * Just * All-Present * Faithful

*Wrathful * Gracious * Lawgiver

My answers can be found in the back of the book. Feel free to compare answers. As you study your Bible you will find these attributes and more!

UNMASKED

The Courage to Be You

Mo Brooks

Season Press

Part 1

How to
UNMASK

A mask is defined as a covering for all or part of the face, worn to conceal one's true identity. A mask is a false, fake, and phony you.

Allow Me to Unmask

I don't know about you, but I don't like it when people tell me what to do without telling me how to do it. So, before I tell you to take off your mask, I want to share what led to me taking off mine. An apple can't be an orange no matter how hard it tries. I should know...

I have attended church my entire life. My grandma was on the Mother Board and my grandfather was a deacon. I attended Sunday school and was baptized at the age of eight. I believed in God. I felt I knew Him so well I could test Him every night by asking Him to wake me up at a certain time every morning. I would choose times like 6:41 a.m. or 3:57 a.m. And every morning, He proved Himself faithful to my request and I would say, "Thank you Lord for waking me up." As a disclaimer I do not advise anyone to test God as I did as a naive child.

As I became a teenager I was given the *choice* of going to church so I popped in and out of church as I pleased. I wore the mask of Christianity by pretending to live as a Christian. I wore the mask of Good Student, Happy Guy, Ladies' Man (that may have been true), Baller, and to adults, an overall Good Young Man. In reality I was living a hellish lifestyle and was struggling in many areas concerning my faith, education, relationships and life! People knew me by the masks I wore around them. I did not want to disappoint anyone. Nobody *really* knew who I was.

I said in words that I was a Christian, but my actions, thoughts and words proved otherwise. We tend to view sex, smoking, drinking and cussing as BIG sins. Well, I did all that and more throughout middle and high school. But no adult really knew because I wore masks. And if they did know, they did not confront me or try to stop me in my sin. Shame on them. I often wonder had I died as a teenager would I have gone to heaven? I thank God I didn't have to find out.

I tell you this not for glory but to show you the masks I use to wear. People like my parents, church members and other adults assumed I was living a Christian lifestyle because I knew how to act in church and around adults. But their assumptions were wrong because it was all for show. While I put on the mask of Christianity for show, others take *off* their mask of Christianity to save their life, not their soul.

News has focused on the Islamic extremist group known as ISIS. This terrorist group based in the Middle East is notorious for beheading Christians. Before they cut off their victim's head, they ask the person to admit or deny if they are a follower of Christ. Those who admit are immediately beheaded.

Those who deny may suffer beheading when they put on a mask to cover up their true Christian identity to avoid persecution.

Now this is a little on the extreme side, but when we sin because we do not want to be criticized by the world, we do the same thing as the group who denied Christ. So we are dealing with two types of people in this book. First, those who do not know Christ, but pretend to know Him by putting on masks that make them look good by their own works. Secondly, those who know Christ but pretend not to know Him in front of certain (worldly) people so they can fit in.

The root cause of our masks could stem from the hurt of an absent parent, abuse, neglect, a generational cruse, fear or wrong teaching. For me it was important to find the root of my masks to prevent even bigger issues returning in my life. I keep asking, "Why do I keep struggling with this so much?" I had a lot of negative experiences and have since forgiven all who hurt me because I know how much God has forgiven me.

Where it all began

I grew up witnessing my dad abuse my mother physically, verbally and emotionally. I was exposed to sexual images early in life (my parents didn't know this), and saw substance abuse as a generational curse in my family. I witnessed poverty, cancer and death to those in my family who were addicted to alcohol and smoking.

We do not have time to dig up all my roots, but I encourage you to know yours. Find out those imperfect things that took place in your life while you were growing up and the history of your family. This may help you understand the struggles you may be having.

Now, I do not want to make it seem like my entire childhood was horrible. My parents loved me and I had a great support system growing up. I had a lot of good memories and can tell you so many stories of family vacations, gatherings and the hilarious times we spent together. I could go on and on about great life skills and lessons my parents taught me. But in my case it was the negative root experiences that led to life-changing struggles and me wearing many masks.

At the age of 14, I received one of the biggest emotional wounds a young man can feel. My dad stabbed my mother three times and nearly killed her. That traumatizing event impacted my life in ways I could not comprehend and I still do not fully understand. It was at an age when I knew one scripture, mainly because it was always repeated in church. I never opened my Bible to search for it myself; but I just heard it said over and over again—*God will not put more on you than you can bear* (1 Cor. 10:13).

When my family and I were at the hospital with my mother, I was the only one who was not teary-eyed. I looked my little brother in the eye and said, "She cannot die Bro' because God cannot put too much on us that we cannot bear." I knew we could not handle my mom dying and my dad being in prison for the rest of his life. The faithfulness of God came through and she lived by what the doctor pronounced as a miracle. Even if my mother had passed away that night, I know that God would have helped us get through it, eventually.

That Scripture held me for that night and I was truly unmasked at that moment in time. When I say I was unmasked, I mean that I was not worried about pleasing anyone but God. Nothing else mattered. Popularity did not matter. Trying to fit in did not matter. Acting happy did not matter. At that time, I was being who God created me to be and I had no fear of letting it show. I was praying, broken and sad.

After that traumatic experience it seemed like my life started a slow road downhill. I began wearing more masks than ever. However, when trouble hit my front door, I took off all of my masks in an attempt to be the best Christ follower I could. But, as soon as trouble appeared to be gone I put my masks back on to try to please others.

I was in a lot of pain all throughout high school and I just smoked weed and Black & Mild cigars, hoping it would ease the pain. I was highly upset that I did not get into the college I desired. I was upset that so many of my peers were doing something with their life and I was not. A year after high school, I hit rock bottom. I was depressed, hurt and terrified about my future and not a soul knew because of the masks I wore. Little did I know, change was coming. But before the masks could come off I had to break a bad habit. Smoking weed (marijuana) put me into zombie mode and my friends were not helping me get closer to God or succeed on any level. The mask I wore was to please them.

I had a best friend who I had known for nearly seventeen years. This friend and I were really close until I broke into his apartment and stole his cousin's Xbox 360. The sad part is, I already had one just like it! I had viewed myself as a loyal person, until that day. The police were called to my apartment to search for the item because two people saw me commit the crime. When the police arrived they did not find anything except the black game controller, which was the only thing I did not have with my game.

My best friend called me and asked what time I was going to be home.

I knew something was not right so I did not show up at 6:30 p.m. like I told him I would. Instead, I showed up to my apartment complex around 10 p.m. to get the Xbox from its hiding place in my broken-down car. I walked to his apartment around the corner and returned the stolen Xbox 360 with tears in my eyes. I apologized and hoped to receive their forgiveness.

But I had betrayed a friend and he made it clear that he could not hang with me anymore. He was loyal at heart, but I knew it would take years for him to forgive me. He expressed that he still loved me like a brother. No one knew it, but after that I cried for days. I asked God to help me stop smoking weed because it was killing me and I knew I would not have done something that stupid had I not been under the influence of drugs. Smoking was ruining my life in ways I could not comprehend at the time.

When my mom found out that I stole my friend's Xbox, she came into my bedroom, looked me straight in the eye and asked, "Who are you? You are not my son! I do not know who you are!" I had been wearing a lot of masks in front of my mom and even she did not recognize me. I wore the mask of her perfect little angel, sober and productive around her. But all of that was a lie and that night she saw my mask. I had never felt so convicted. I knew God was speaking to me through my mother. All I could do was cry, cry and cry some more. When I asked God for help and confessed my wrong doings, He took the "Lying-to-my-mother" mask off. She was now able to help me because she knew who I really was.

The same summer I stole from my best friend I went to visit my dad's family in Lansing, Michigan. Five years earlier, it was my cousin there who taught me how to smoke weed. He had just gotten his own apartment and we decided to smoke some weed. While we were smoking my grandmother surprisingly walked in.

She came straight over to me and said, "Boy, you smoke?"

"Yes, ma'am."

She did not say another word and just left the apartment. I was crushed. I did not want my grandma to view me in that light. I started smoking weed to fit in with my family, friends and peers to be "cool." But for my grandmother to see me with that mask on hurt me because I knew that was not the real me.

I felt naked and ashamed when I looked into my grandma's eyes and I could not live with her viewing me as the person in that mask. That "Cool" mask was worn for certain people and my grandmother was not one of them. Those who knew I smoked thought I was joking when I declared to stop. I was so convicted by God through my grandmother's disappointment that nothing was going to change my mind.

After countless episodes of my friends pressuring me to smoke, I told them I would not be coming around them anymore. When the masks of the thief and weed smoker were taken off, my life changed. The masks I had worn to cover up my true identity in Christ were coming off before God and the entire world.

The Big Change

On December 31, 2008 (nearly six months after I stopped smoking), I decided to go to a party to celebrate the New Year. That same night my older cousin from the east coast came to town and asked me to go to church with him. I had money in my pocket, liquor and fun on my mind. But, for some odd reason I told him, yes I would go to church.

During the church service, I felt like I was the only person in the sanctuary. I felt that every word that came out of the preacher's mouth was spoken directly to me. I surrendered to Jesus that night in tears and praise. I thought being caught up in the emotions of the experience that night would fade. However I woke up the next morning with my first thoughts on Jesus. I made a commitment to God to read one chapter of the Bible each day and to attend my home church every Sunday.

I believed God was happy with my commitment because it was more than I had been doing in the past. My life had taken a 180-degree turn. I began to unmask before the God of the universe and repent of every sin that was revealed to me as I read and began to personalize the Bible. Repent once means to change your mind, stop doing the sin you are doing and start obeying God. I was working hard to take off the remaining masks that I had been wearing for years. I wanted one thing and one thing only—to live an unmasked life pleasing to God.

My home church was Mt. Zion Baptist Church in Kalamazoo, Michigan where I found myself keeping the promise I made to God. Every Sunday I would hear a relevant Word from God that would challenge, encourage and inspire me to continue to grow In Christ. I also continued to read at least one chapter a day.

Seeing my mask come off was amazing and shocking. I never thought I would be able to stop smoking, having premarital sex, cussing, drinking, or changing my close friends. I will admit, some masks were hard to take off. Much prayer, focus, repentance, counsel and discipline was required to stop me from doing these and other sinful habits.

Due to the great teaching, preaching and leadership of my pastor and church family I discovered my purpose, passion and gifts. I grew in my Christian walk and was called to preach the Gospel of Jesus the Christ. I served as a deacon and later was licensed as an associate minister in November of 2012. Today, I primarily serve our youth in addition to several other ministries. My family, emotional, spiritual, social, financial, and educational life have been changed because I allowed Jesus to take over my life.

Jesus changed my life through His Word, His people and just getting to know Him. Everyone has their own story of how God pursued them and entered their life. Do not be afraid of the mistakes you have made in the past. Jesus died for every sin and He gives us the strength to kill our sin habits day by day through His Word and the Holy Spirit. Without my sins and mistakes and how God came into my life, I would not be where I am today. This may sound strange but stealing my friend's Xbox 360, and my grandma catching me in the act of smoking, were two of the best things that ever happened in my life.

If Jesus can forgive my sin, free me from my addictions and cleanse me from the inside out, He can do the same for you. Please do not get it twisted; the Holy Spirit is working on me every day to be more like Christ. You and I must build our relationship with God and become the Young Courageous Christians He called us to be.

I believe that you may desire to be a Young Courageous Christian but may not know how, or are afraid to take off your mask. The Bible can be intimidating to open up and read. You may not know where to start. I felt the same way. But, the more I read the Word and other Christian books that pointed back to the Word, the more it helped tremendously.

What is a mask?

On Halloween, people all over America wear different masks, pretending to be someone they are really not. Think about your favorite Halloween costume throughout the years. My favorite was the Freddy Kruger costume with the mask, hat and claw. While I had that mask on nobody could really tell who I really was. I could only be identified if I took off the mask. I wish the only time we wore masks were on Halloween.

We wear masks every day. They are masks in the form of different beliefs, behaviors and attitudes. I think it is fair to say that many people wear some type of mask to hide their true identity from certain people—and even

God. Why? Is it fear or a lack of trust? Do we fear people will not accept us for who we are? Or do we put on different masks because we do not know who we really are?

On a first date we rarely let anyone see who we really are. The goal is to try to impress the other person, even at the cost of lying or acting unlike our true self. The fear of rejection leads some to put on the mask of being smooth, popular, tough, non-aggressive or patient. These masks can be interchanged within seconds.

Are you being the person you claim to be in front of your family, friends, classmates, co-workers and church members? Do you claim to be a Christian, good student, good child, loyal, honest and nice even though deep down inside that is just not who you are? Masks serve as a method of protection from criticism, correction, rejection and the truth.

When I was thirteen years old, my mom asked me if I used profanity. I replied, "No Mom, of course I don't cuss. I am a Christian." As soon as I left the house, guess what? I started to curse like a sailor. Around my friends I put on my "Cool/Fit in," mask to cover my true identity in Christ.

My parents did not know who I really was because I was not honest with them. Because of that they could not help or parent me effectively. Do you see how a simple thing like cursing was a mask that covered up my true identity in Christ? I did not want to be rejected or talked about, so I put on a mask in front of a group of people to fit in.

There is nothing wrong with being accepted and loved. But, teens and young adults should not have to put on a mask just to maintain friendships. They know they should not be cursing, having premarital sex, or skipping class. Some participate in that behavior to put on the mask of popularity, which drives them to make wrong decisions.

Even when we struggle with a crisis, bad habits, addictions or anything that is difficult in life, we may put on the mask of perfection and pretend everything is good. At school, work, church or wherever we may go, we have a smile on our face, but even that smile is a mask. When there is pain in our hearts we often put on our mask of perfection to cover it up. On the outside things seem as if everything is okay. But the truth is we need help or someone to talk to. The longer the mask of fake perfection stays on, the worse it gets. Many marriages look great on the outside. They have children, good jobs and may even attend church. Then all of the sudden, you hear they are getting a divorce. They were wearing a mask of perfection and that everything was good on the outside, while beneath the mask everything was being torn apart.

Let's get transparent. Think of some masks you wear. I personally have worn a lot of masks throughout my life. By the grace of God I have destroyed a lot of masks as well. I would be lying if I told you I am mask-free. Every day is a fight to live an unmasked life. It is a fight to allow my identity in Christ shine forth despite what others may think or say about me.

To be unmasked before God means you can live unmasked before any human. One way to unmask before God is to remember this Scripture: *If we confess our sins, He is faithful and just to forgive us our sins and to cleanse us from all unrighteousness* (1 John 1:9). This Scripture means we tell God, in prayer, about the specific sin and mask that we have been wearing. After all, He already knows. Join me in taking off our masks and be Young Courageous Christians!

WORK Is a Must

Most likely you grew up in homes where your parents or someone responsible for you bought most of your clothing. If you were lucky they bought new electronics or other things you desired. Now, how many of those things have you broken, lost or simply ruined? Especially with shoes? I don't know about you but I cannot even count how many valuable things my parents bought that I have lost or ruined. My mom would eventually buy new shoes when mine looked bad. To her, my appearance was a reflection on her as a parent.

Parents, or whoever provided for you, may have gotten on your case about keeping your things clean and safe. Do you know why? Because they worked hard and sacrificed so you could have and enjoy those things. Some parents worked long hours, completed college and experienced some type of stress just to be able to provide needs and wants for their children. All they asked you to do was protect, watch over and take care of the things they bought you.

As you begin to work to buy the things that you want you will feel as if you have earned your paycheck. You follow the instruction of your boss, wake up early, stay up late and do the things you do not feel like doing, just to get that paycheck. After you cash the check you go to buy something that you desire (correct me if I am wrong on twitter @mo_brooks). There is something different when you make that purchase. You vow to protect, watch over and take care of the item you bought because you have worked for it. You no longer treat your clothing, shoes or electronics any type of way.

Why is that not the case when others purchased the things you desired? Because you did not put in the work to buy it. I am afraid that most Christians are not protecting, watching over or taking care of their Christian faith because they have not put in the work! A lot of young Christians are relying on their parents, grandparents and spiritual leaders to have faith for them but never get to the point of putting in the work to have genuine faith themselves. Putting in the work means studying the Scriptures for yourself, cutting out sinful habits, asking questions about Christianity, building a prayer life and putting your faith to work through obedience to Christ.

Learn who God is and do what it takes to ensure your belief in Him. It is hard to appreciate the grace that has been given to you and the blessing you have without putting in some work and really knowing the work Jesus has put in for you. I do not know about you but I have put in too much work to ruin my Christian witness for some foolish sin that does nothing for me anyway.

I will guard my faith not only because of the work Jesus has put in for me, but because of the work He has allowed me to put in through His grace and sacrifice on the cross. Please do not get me wrong. The work that you end up putting into your Christian walk is an expression of God's grace.

Part 2

UNMASKing
Your Potential

There are some things you have to do and have to avoid in order to unmask your potential. When you have on masks you are hindering your potential. Your potential has to do with your future and all God has created you to be.

When you unmask your potential, you will realize how awesome you are. Your potential is the stuff in you that has not been released. It is your dreams and the goals that have yet to be accomplished. It is the places that you have not been yet. It is the lives that have not been changed yet because of the unique gift that God has given you.

The Power of the Word
For the Word of God is living and powerful
-Hebrews 4:12-

If being a Young Courageous Christian were easy everyone would be one. But that is not the case. To you it may seem impossible to live for Jesus, change your lifestyle and keep the faith for your entire life. I am here to tell you that you can do it because Jesus died so you could have that opportunity. It is in the Word of God where we find out all things are possible with Him. If you want to fulfill your potential then you have to unmask your potential.

I want you to understand two things about the Word of God. First, the Word is powerful. God uses His Word to change habits, generational curses, lives and whatever else needs purging in your life. *In the beginning was the Word and the Word was with God and the Word was God* (John 1:1). In the Word is love, power, knowledge, grace, mercy, the wrath of God and so much more.

Secondly, the Word is a seed. When you read the Word of God you are always planting a seed in your soul and mind. Do not get discouraged if your life does not completely change in two days after spending time with God in His Word. A seed takes time to grow and mature. Just like a seed planted in the ground, it needs sunlight, water and good soil to grow. Every time you hear or do the Word of God you are growing a seed.

As you go through your personal study, open yourself to the teaching, preaching and praising of the Lord, growth is taking place. I don't care who you are; you can't recognize substantial growth overnight. But, someone who may not have seen you in a while will see it. The Word is powerful and works in a way that you will not understand immediately. Stick with your commitment even when the going gets tough.

Unmask

Change your perspective on the Bible. The Word of God is not just another book. It is the living Word of God (Hebrews 4:12). Know that you have potential. But the only way to unmask that potential is through the Word of God. Please do not waste your God-given potential because you refuse to study and obey the Word.

Additional Scriptures to study:

Psalm 107:20
Psalm 18:30, 138:2
Proverbs 30:5
Isaiah 40:6-8, 55:8-11
Jeremiah 23:29
Matthew 8:8 (but read entire story)
Matthew 24:35,
Mark 4:1-20
Luke 6:46-49
John 1:1-14
Romans 1:16, 10:17,
James 1:21-25
Hebrews 4:12
1 Peter 1:22-25

Commitment:

_____
_____
_____
_____
_____
_____

Renew Your Mind
A mind is a terrible thing to waste
-Malcolm X-

Our mind is shaped by how we were raised, what we watch, listen to and read. Just because we were raised a certain way does not make certain things right. Some of you were raised with the belief that if someone cursed you out, you had a right to curse back; no disrespect would be tolerated.

The Word of God has different instructions: *Blessed those who Curse you* (Matthew 5:44). God wants us to renew our mind. Renewing your mind has to happen through the Word.

Renewing your mind is all about your way of thinking. You have control over your thoughts. The secret to overriding your negative or sinful thoughts, is through speaking out loud. The gateways to the mind are our eyes, ears, mouth and nose. What are you watching, listening to, and reading? To renew our mind we must be aware of what goes into our gateways. If you could grade your God thoughts from 1-10 (10 being the best) how would you rank them? As long as we are living we will have to continue to renew our mind. None of us are at a 10!

I like to watch the ESPN Sports Network. There is nothing in Scripture that says, "thou shall not watch ESPN." But I know, for me, watching more than an hour of ESPN can draw me away from the time I have committed to spend with Christ each day. Most days, I do not watch ESPN because I know it will take away from my time with Christ. I am not telling you to never watch television, listen to music or watch a movie.

I am telling you that you have to carefully guard your mind, *Therefore gird up the loins of your mind, be sober, and rest your hope fully upon the grace that is to be brought to you at the revelation of Jesus Christ* (1 Peter 1:13-16). Anything that draws you away from Christ—whether morally right or wrong, is very dangerous and must be dealt with. Renew your mind.

Unmask

Write down the things you listen to, watch and read that are ungodly, meaning they do not help you get closer to God. If you need more space get an extra sheet of paper. Be specific and name the show, song, artist, etc.

_____

_____

_____

_____

Now, what can you replace those things with things that will help you get closer to Jesus and His goals for your life? Set out times to spend with the Lord. Remember, to put in the work to unmask.

_____

_____

_____

_____

Additional scriptures to study:

Romans 8:5-8, 12:1-2
Ephesians 4:20-24
Philippians 2:1-5
1 Corinthians 2:10-16
2 Corinthians 10:3-6
Colossians 3:1-17
1 Peter 1:13

Commitment:

_____

_____

_____

_____

_____

_____

Change
To improve is to change; to be perfect is to change often.
-Winston Churchill-

Change can be difficult when we are comfortable with the bad habits we created (1Corinthians 5:6). Most people hate change because it pushes them out of their comfort zone. Change causes us to do something different without knowing the outcome. If you are going to grow in Christ you will have to change!

As humans grow from infants to adults, change is inevitable. Change is vital if you are going to be a Young Courageous Christian. Repentance is the key to change. I am talking about change in the context of adjusting your lifestyle so you may be more like Christ. In order to unlock your potential you will have to change.

Unmask

You know what changes you have to make to be more like Christ and align with His word. Write down what changes you need to make. Read them every day. Whatever your change is, write it down and speak it (Habakkuk 2:2-4, Proverbs 23:7, Proverbs 18:21 and 2 Corinthians 4:13). Remember to be real honest with yourself and what you need to change. Just keep it real!

(Examples: stop smoking, attend church weekly, stop thinking negative about yourself or stop cutting) _____

_____
_____
_____
_____

Additional Scriptures to study:

Luke 13:2-5
Romans 12:1-2
2 Timothy 3:16

* Note: As you read Bible stories pay attention how God will ask people to change.

Commitment:

_____
_____
_____
_____
_____
_____

Success
This Book of the Law shall not depart from your mouth, but you shall meditate in it day and night, that you may observe to do according to all that is written in it. For then you will make your way prosperous, and then you will have good success (Joshua 1:8).
-God-

Write down what you want people to say about you at your Homegoing celebration (when you die). I know we do not like to think about death but I am just keeping it real.

_____

_____

_____

_____

Most likely, the things you wrote down on your list are *your* true definition of success. Did it include the amount of money you made? The things you owned? That you were a good parent or child, a loving person who kept promises, and/or a person of good reputation?

Your definition of success may be totally different than God's definition. God has a purpose for you. Success begins when you are born and when you find out the reason you were born. Fulfilling your purpose will lead you to the success that will fill you with peace and joy. Everyone will not have the same definition of success. Your definition is based on your purpose, gifts and talents.

Can you find your dreams, goals and aspirations in the Word of God? Does it have anything to do with winning souls and changing lives? Does your definition have anything to do with being like Christ? If the answers to these questions are no then you have a distorted and worldly view of success.

All I am trying to say is make sure your career goals and desires are in line with the Master's. God has a plan for your life but that plan is revealed through obeying Scripture.

I beseech you therefore, brethren, by the mercies of God, that you present your bodies a living sacrifice, holy, acceptable to God, which is your reasonable service. And do not be conformed to this world, but be transformed by the renewing of your mind, that you may prove what is that good and acceptable and perfect will of God.
Romans 12:1-2

Trust in the Lord with all your heart, And lean not on your own understanding; In all your ways acknowledge Him, And He shall direct your paths. Do not be wise in your own eyes; Fear the Lord and depart from evil.
Proverbs 3:5-6

Studying the Word alone is not the end goal; it's applying the Word of God on a consistent basis. Application of the scriptures is what get results and provokes life change; nothing more and nothing less. If you do not apply Scripture to your everyday life then you can forget about unmasking your God potential.

Unmask

Change your definition of success. Find out what God wants you to do and then do it! Then you will be successful in the sight of God, mankind and yourself. Write down your goals, dreams and definition of success. Now make decisions based of that definition.

Additional Scriptures to study:

Joshua 1:1-8
Psalm 1:1-3
Psalm 37: 1-40
Proverbs 14:12, 16:9, 25
Ecclesiastes 10:10
Galatians 6: 7-10
Ephesians 2:10

Commitment:

_____
_____
_____
_____
_____
_____

Discipline
*Now no chastening (discipline) seems to be joyful for the present,
but painful; nevertheless, afterward it yields the peaceable fruit of
righteousness to those who have been trained by it.*
Hebrews 12:11
-God-

I cannot remember where I heard this definition of discipline, but it always stuck with me: *Discipline is doing what needs to be done right now.* I think that is a powerful statement. So, the lack of discipline means you are *not* doing what needs to be done at the current moment. Jesus called His followers disciples for a reason. The root of disciple is *discipline.* In order to follow Jesus you need discipline. You will have to do what needs to be done at the moment.

Discipline declares, "I need to do this instead of that right now." Christian discipline is created through developing Christian habits. It is said that it takes twenty-one days of doing something to make it a habit. Once a habit is formed it becomes a part of who you are and your lifestyle. It is not enough to say that we are Christians, but our lifestyle must prove that we Christian.

One of the teenagers in my Fulfillment Hour (Sunday School) class asked, "Can you be a disciple if you do not do what disciples do?" I replied, "Can a cheerleader be a cheerleader without cheering? Can a rapper be a rapper without rhyming? Can basketball players call themselves, ballers without playing the game? Can a swimmer be called a swimmer if they never hit the pool?"

You cannot find anywhere in Scripture where someone was following the Lord without doing what He commands. You cannot be a disciple without doing what disciples do! In order to do what disciples do, you must have discipline.

Unmask

This is one of the harder topics. Discipline is painful at times and takes time to build up. In order to address our discipline issue we must be honest about the areas we are not disciplined in. Can you recognize those areas?

Is it going to sleep and waking up at a certain time? Is it spending time with our Lord each morning or night? Is it not partying on Saturday night so you can attend Church on Sunday? Is it watching pornography?

This list could go on, and on, but please think about the areas you need to increase your discipline. Now, make some commitments as it pertains to those things.

Additional Scripture to study:

Matthew 28:16-19
Luke 9:23
John 8:31
1 Corinthians 9:24-27
Galatians 5:16-25

Commitment:

_____
_____
_____
_____
_____

Procrastination
The longer you wait to do something you should do now, the greater the odds that you will never actually do it.
-John Maxwell-

Procrastination is disciplines' biggest enemy. Procrastination is such a hindrance because of this phrase: "I HAVE TIME!" Things get put off because we believe we have time to accomplish our goals. This bites us in the butt most of the time because the truth is we do not have time. If we had time the word procrastination would not exist. Why do we wait to do what needs to be done at the last moment? Procrastination is deadly and has hurt a lot of believers from living a life that is unmasked.

God gives us commandments because He is Lord and that is what He has a right to do. Waiting to obey God gives room to doubt and allow negative thoughts and Satan to prevent you from following the Lord's instructions. Please do not believe, the statement: "I will really follow Jesus when I get older because I have time...I need to have fun now."

Jesus is not a toy that you pick up when you are ready to play. Jesus is worthy of our lives because He died for us. Jesus is Lord and in Him are all our needs. Putting Jesus off until tomorrow shows a lack of discipline and needs to be addressed in your life immediately. Do not give the devil all of your young and high-energy days. God wants that time to work for Him.

Why are you trying to wait until you are older to live for Christ? I believe that young people have a special influence because of their youth. Not saying that older people do not have a huge influence on young people but there is something powerful about young people living for God.

Unmask

Make a list of things you are putting off until later. Be real. Is it reading your Bible every day? Attending church? Doing your homework on time? Forgiving someone who hurt you? Once you identified your procrastination areas, read the additional scriptures and make a commitment to repent.

_____

_____

_____

_____

Additional Scripture to study:

Psalm 39:4-5
102:3 & 11
John 9:4
Romans 13:11
Ephesians 5:15-17
1 John 1:9

Commitment:

_____

_____

_____

_____

The Power of the Christian
*But Jesus looked at them and said to them, "With men this is impossible,
but with God all things are possible" (Matthew 19:26).*
-Jesus-

Christians are powerful because of the strength of God who dwells within us. Every temptation, every problem, every circumstance can be dealt with when God's Word is working in our lives. Think about that for a moment. Christians learn to have peace, joy, love, patience and the ability to overcome anything that they face through Christ.

God gives the believer in Christ the power, energy and wisdom to do the hard things. The number-one reason (in my opinion) people do not live courageously for God is due to the lifestyle change that will take place. People do not want to get rid of their sin, or they may think it is impossible to get rid of their sin. So, they suppress hearing from God.

When Jesus becomes your Lord you will find yourself hating the sin you once loved. God changes the believer's heart as it is written: *Then I will sprinkle clean water on you, and you shall be clean; I will cleanse you from all your filthiness and from all your idols. I will give you a new heart and put a new spirit within you; I will take the heart of stone out of your flesh and give you a heart of flesh. I will put My Spirit within you and cause you to walk in My statutes, and you will keep My judgments and do them"*(Ezekiel 36:25-27).

Truthfully, a lot of people do not want a new heart because they are in love with sin and hate God. Not too many people will say that they hate God, but their actions say differently. At one point of time we all were enemies of God. Jesus died on the cross so we could be reconciled (joined back together with) Christ.

Jesus' desire is that we may have a relationship with Him and that we carry out His will with His power and authority. We are representatives for Christ. Since we represent Christ, He will give us everything we need to get His work done. I am not talking directly about doing all types of miracles because I think the biggest miracle is our salvation. Christ will give us the power to overcome every temptation, every problem and every circumstance so that we may protect our witness. You have power if you are living for Jesus.

Unmask

Do you have the, "I can't help it" syndrome? Do you say, "I have no control over my sinful habits." Does every circumstance that happens in your life get you down and depressed? If so, check your obedience and relationship with Christ. Repent from the sin that is leading to death, spiritually and possibly physically. Know what comes with your salvation. Know the power you have through Christ. The real you is powerful, unstoppable and can do all things through Christ. Please do not put on a mask that says something different.

Additional Scriptures to study:

John 14:12-14
Acts 1:8
Romans 8:37
Ephesians 3:20
Philippians 4:13
1 John 4:4

Commitment:

_____
_____
_____
_____
_____
_____

God thinks about you
How precious also are Your thoughts to me, O God!
How great is the sum of them!
-Psalm 139:17-

God is love (1 John 4:8) but hates sin. God's anger is focused on the sinner because He wants to save you. I hope you do not shut the book and get angry because of that statement. This is why it is so important to know who God is and His attributes. The world, through movies and media, has created this all-loving God who loves everyone, is forgiving of all, and that everyone who has lived a decent life is going to heaven. That is a trick and a lie! It is important for us to know that God righteously and lovingly hates sin and does not give anyone a "pass."

Yes, God was very angry about my past ways and I do not blame Him. God was furious with me because I was one with my sin. I thought sinful thoughts all the time. I did sinful things all the time. And the good I thought I was doing was not good in His sight.

But we are all like an unclean thing, And all our righteousnesses are like filthy rags; We all fade as a leaf, And our iniquities, like the wind, Have taken us away, (Isaiah 64:6).

It is important to know that if you are not a Christian and have not accepted Jesus as Lord through repenting from sin and obeying His Will, then you have a huge problem with God. I would be a liar to say that God is cool with everyone. If that were the case, there would be no need for salvation, a renewed mind, repentance or a changed heart. None of the Christian doctrine would make sense if God were okay with sinners.

I am the first to admit that I did not like hearing that God had an issue with me. I felt like God should love me and bless me because He is God. But, that harsh truth changed my life. I pray that it will prick your heart and cause you to make a decision about God. If you are a sinner you need to know that God is not pleased with you.

God is love and He desires that everyone should be saved (1 Peter 3:9). God is always thinking about our future and ways to reveal Himself to us. He thinks about you so much, as stated in Jeremiah 29:11:

For God cannot think of evil or know evil. "For I know the thoughts that I think toward you, says the Lord, thoughts of peace and not of evil, to give you a future and a hope.

This also is stated in 2 Corinthians 5:21, which states: *For He made Him who knew no sin to be sin for us, that we might become the righteousness of God in Him*. Jesus died for you and He loves you. Know that you are on the mind of God. God is here to help you unmask, repent and assist you with your entire life.

Unmask

God is thinking about you and your future. As a matter of fact, God thought about you before you were born. He has a huge plan for your life. This is important to know because it lets you know that you have purpose and meaning. God loves you so much and wants the best for you. Just know and say, "I am on the mind of the Almighty God who created the heavens and the earth."

Additional Scriptures to study:

Jeremiah 11:29
Psalm 5:5, 11:5, 40:5, 139:17
John 3:36

Commitment:

_____
_____
_____
_____
_____
_____

Part 3

UNMASKing
Everyday Life

Being a Christian is an everyday practice. Sundays are not the only day when we should read our Word or pray. Jesus is worthy to be praised, honored and lived for every day.

You Are What You Eat

The phrase above is very simple but powerful. It is a phrase that many have heard and will agree with. The problem with this phrase is that people know it is true but will not conform their lives to this truth. The issue is not knowing the truth, but not having the discipline to make a change that may save their life.

You are what you eat is so true, and if you have not grown to realize that yet, you will as you continue to age. When you eat a lot of fatty or sugary foods you may become sluggish and sleepy all the time. This may lead to disease over time. Not only are you what you eat, but exercise is a huge component when trying to live healthy. Your diet and exercise habits can either help you live a long healthy life or destroy your body earlier than intended. A lot of people find it hard to be energized, run when needed or be healthy because of what they consume on a regular bases.

I believe it is hard for Christians to live for Christ because of what we consume on a regular bases. We have been introduced to this culture of going to church on Sunday and Wednesdays to hear the Word. So, we spend about four hours in church learning about Jesus each week and the other 164 hours of the week listening to ungodly messages/music, viewing ungodly shows/billboards and being preached to and taught by ungodly friends. Can you see the disparity?

Christianity is not about going to church on Sundays and Wednesdays only to hear the Word and feel good about yourself. It is about an everyday devotion to the Lord. If you feed your flesh more than your spirit, it will always and forever be a struggle to follow Jesus. It is a struggle for me when I feed my flesh more than my spirit. If I find myself watching too much television or being social too much during the week, I also struggle with sharing my faith, I get depressed or even angry, which could lead to the potential of me risking the chance of putting on masks that I have not worn in a while.

The healthiest spiritual food we can consume is the Word of God! You just do not eat physical food twice a week. This is where that discipline kicks in. We attend Prayer meetings, Bible study and an effort to obey Christ and be a witness through our lifestyle. The best spiritual exercises you can do is to be a witness and make disciples.

So, if you are finding it hard to do spiritual things then we must watch what we are eating on a daily bases. Matthew 4:4 says, *But He answered and said, It is written, Man shall not live by bread alone, but by every word that proceeds from the mouth of God*. God wants you to eat, consume and live by His word.

Why do I have to study my Bible constantly?

Each time you open your Bible, God has a huge smile on His face. He loves you so much. He is pleased when you are looking to Him for answers or just to get closer to Him. God also commands us to study in 2 Timothy 2:15 where it says, *Be Diligent (study) to show thyself approved unto God, a work man that needth not to be ashamed but rightly dividing the word of truth*.

According to this text alone we should study our Bible for three reasons:

1. **It is a command.** Remember that God is perfect and loving, He will never tell you to do something that will harm you or that He has not done Himself through the life of Jesus. The text says, Study. It did not say, "If you *want* to study."

   Studying provides you with knowledge of who God is, who you are (or are supposed to be) what God expects (how to please Him) and instructions to follow (2 Timothy 3:16). You cannot obey/follow Jesus if you do not know what His word says. Studying will help you retain information to apply it to your life, as stated in Psalm 119:11: *Your word I have hidden in my heart, That I might not sin against You*.

2. **To do the works of a Christian without shame**. How can you do something when you do not know how to do it? The Bible gives us instructions on how to be the Christians/disciple we want to be. But if we do not study then we will not know what to do. This will also help us not be shameful because we know that God is faithful and He will keep every promise.

   God has a purpose for you and a lot of that purpose will be birth through studying the Scripture. When we go to work for God, wherever we are, we want to do it with excellence, the right heart and motive. Studying unlocks that door to work for our Lord correctly and confidently.

3. **Rightly dividing the Word of Truth.** As young people we have to be very careful in what we listen to and watch concerning the Word of God. Since the beginning of time people have been twisting the Word of God for their own sinful pleasures:

As also in all his epistles, speaking in them of these things, in which are some things hard to understand, which untaught and unstable people twist to their own destruction, as they do also the rest of the Scripture. You therefore, beloved, since you know this beforehand, beware lest you also fall from your own steadfastness, being led away with the error of the wicked; but grow in the grace and knowledge of our Lord and Savior Jesus Christ. To Him be the glory both now and forever. Amen. (2 Peter 3:16-18).

Going to a Biblical teaching-and-preaching church is so important. That is why I encourage you to get to know the Word yourself so God can show you the truth and when others preach or teach from the Bible you can have some understanding to know if it is truth or not. Also, as a witness for Jesus you want to teach people correctly. Sitting under sound teaching, studying throughout the week and having believers around you who can discuss Scripture with will help tremendously with rightly dividing the word of truth.

Here are some Scriptures that support studying your Bible: Matthew 11:25-30 (vs. 29 is the focus) John 1:1-18 (vs. 1-5, 14 and 18 is the focus).

> **Reminder:** Studying the Word of God without application will do you great harm. Please understand that Scripture is to be obeyed and not just memorized or read.

All Scripture is given by inspiration of God, and is profitable for doctrine, for reproof, for correction, for instruction in righteousness, that the man of God may be complete, thoroughly equipped for every good work.
2 Timothy 3:16

To live an unmasked life it is key for you to eat the Word of God through studying and applying it.

How to Study God's Word (3 Steps)

There may be different ways to study the Bible. I particularly like the three different steps on studying your Bible from the book, *The New How to Study Your Bible*, by Kay Arthur, David Arthur and Pete De Lacy. I encourage you to get this book for deeper understanding on how to study. What I gleaned from it follows.

Step One: Observation

Let me ask you a quick question. Why did God drive Adam and Eve out of the Garden of Eden? What did they eat? A lot of people would answer that question, "They ate the apple of the tree." I know it seems small but the text says *fruit* not apple.

Did you see that? If you do not correctly observe the text then the next two steps could be incorrect. It sounds simple but a lot of people ruin correct interpretation of the Bible by not knowing what the Bible says. Observation is getting a bird's-eye view of the text. What does the text say? Do not add or take away a single word. While observing the text you want to look for words that stand out to you or repeated terms within a chapter or book.

Step Two: Interpretation

Interpretation answers the question, what does the text mean? This is the most important step of the three because if you get this step wrong then you leave the door open to incorrect doctrine, which leads to a misrepresentation of Jesus. The main rule to interpretation is: let Scripture interpret Scripture. You cannot take one Scripture and isolate it.

Do you know the historical context of the Scripture? Do you know the setting, culture and people that text is referring to? These things are imperative when attempting to interpret a text. Yes, you will have to ask other believers about certain text to make sure you are interpreting them correctly.

I have asked many questions because I want to make sure I am are rightly dividing the Word of Truth. Ask your pastor, youth minister, teachers and godly parents questions about Scriptures that are not clear to you. Wrestle with the Scripture in prayer. Trust me, one day someone may come to you with questions and you will be able to provide an answer.

It is important that you find the definitions of words you do not know. The Bible's original language is not English, therefore you will have to use a concordance or Bible dictionary to define biblical words. The Old Testament was written in Hebrew and the New Testament was written in Greek and Latin. In the 'additional unmasking tools' section; in the back of the book I have some great tools that can help you do this and some of them are free!

Step Three:

Application answers the questions, "How does the meaning of this passage apply to me?" "What truths am I to embrace/believe, or order my life by?" And what changes should I make in my belief for my life?"

Without this step the other two steps are pointless. An acronym for B.I.B.L.E. is: Basic Instruction Before Leaving Earth. The key word to me is *instruction* because that means we have to follow the direction God gives us through Scripture.

God makes it clear that He wants us to obey His commands. You may not understand every command but understanding will come after trusting God through obedience to Him.

The fear of the Lord is the beginning of wisdom; A good understanding have all those who do His commandments. His praise endures forever.
Psalm 111:10

Just like Blood

I gave blood for the first time in October 2013, during a blood drive at my church. Afterward, I was a little woozy. The more blood you lose the weaker you become. If you lose enough blood your life may be at risk in a hurry. Losing blood is a fairly quick process. A scratch will not affect your health (unless infected) but a gunshot wound needs to be taken care of immediately.

Well, prayer works just like blood in our life. When we have the correct amount of blood flowing and circulating through our bodies we are healthy, vibrant and strong. The Christians who spends time in daily prayer turns out to be healthy, vibrant and strong. Those Christians who do not spend time in daily prayer become weaker in faith by the day. The daily bombardment of temptations that you face can only be won through building a daily prayer life. It is impossible to live an unmasked life without prayer. Studying the

Word and prayer go hand-in-hand. Just begin to study and you will know what I mean.

Jesus was a man of prayer. He prayed before He made big decisions or did work for His Father. It was his daily custom. Jesus is perfect, Holy and has never sinned and He still was a Man of prayer. How much more should we be praying, knowing that Jesus prayed often? Remember God will never ask you to do something that He has not already done through the life of Jesus.

So, what is prayer? Prayer is not a monologue, but a dialogue. Prayer is not just asking God for stuff that you want, but it is a conversation. In Jerimiah 33:3 it reads: *Call upon me and I will answer you and show you great and mighty things, which you do not know.*

Here God says, He will answer you if you call upon Him. Scripture shows a lot of evidence of people talking and listening to God. What does God sound like? God sounds like His Word. God will not tell you anything that goes against His nature or His Word.

I will worship toward Your Holy temple, and praise Your name For Your loving kindness and Your truth; For You have magnified Your word above all Your name.
Psalm 138:2

God speaks to us through His Word, the Holy Spirit, His people, creation and even circumstances. God loves us so much that He wants to be in constant communication. He desires that we run to Him with every need, question or concern. I believe prayer is one of the essential attributes of the Christian. It is not a mere spiritual exercise. Your life (and the lives of others) depends on your prayers and is designed to be done all day long through meditation. Luke 18:1 says, *Man ought to always pray and not lose heart.*

You do not need to be on your knees all day praying. However, we need to be intentionally thinking how we can please God throughout our day. Meditation means to think, speak and do the Word of God. It is not sitting down with your legs crossed. If that were the case God would not tell us to mediate day and night. The Christian who does not pray may lack courage needed to be brave and not conform to this world. This may be the most important chapter of this book. Without a prayer life a Christian may not be getting the "blood" they need to survive.

How do you pray? Jesus teaches His disciples how to pray in Matthew 6:11-14 with the Lord's Prayer. Prayer includes giving thanks to God, praying for His will to be done, ask for forgiveness of sins (repentance) and help to forgive others. Prayer is a dialogue with God. As we pray God will give us directions on how to give thanks, how to do His will, how to ask for forgiveness and forgive others. Remember His directions will come through His Word, Holy Spirit, His people, His creation and even circumstances. Prayers do not get answered just by simply praying. There are two key components that allow God to answer prayer.

The first component that must be present for prayer to be answered is faith. Scripture is clear about having faith *before* prayer takes place. Romans 10:17 declares: *faith comes by hearing and hearing by the Word of God*. I suggest that you study your Word before prayer.

If faith comes by hearing God's Word and you need faith to pray, then I suggest hearing and believing some Word before prayer. Hebrews 11:6 indicates, that you cannot pray if you do not believe that God is who He said He is. That is why it is important that you study the attributes of God and get to know them well. It pleases God that His child prays but it is impossible to please Him without faith (Hebrews 11:6). God leaves no room for a lack of faith.

> *Therefore I say to you, whatever things you ask when you pray,*
> *believe that you receive them, and you will have them*
> **Mark 11:24**

> *If any of you lacks wisdom, let him ask of God, who gives to all*
> *liberally and without reproach, and it will be given to him.*
> *But let him ask in faith, with no doubting, for he who doubts*
> *is like a wave of the sea driven and tossed by the wind.*
> **James 1:5-6**

The second component that must be present for prayer to be answered is the inclusion of God's Will. If your prayer is lined up with the Will of God, He will answer that prayer. Now, that is exciting! A good parent will freely give anything that their child asks if it is in the will of that parent (Matthew 7:7-11 and Romans 8:32). If you ask your parent something that contradicts their will they will not give you what you asked for. God wants to answer our prayers but it must line up with His will.

Now this is the confidence that we have in Him, that if we ask anything according to His will, He hears us. And if we know that He hears us, whatever we ask, we know that we have the petitions that we have asked of Him.
1 John 5:13-14

The Word promises us that God will hear us if we ask according to His Will and if He hears us He will answer us. *He will not hear those who have iniquity in their heart.*
Psalm 66:19

That is why it is important to ask for forgiveness of sin and repent. In order to know the will of God, we must study the Scriptures. The only thing that will block the hearing of God is sin.

Grind Time

I often refer to my walk with Christ as an everyday grind. I say this because every day I am striving to please God more and more. Every day there are different struggles and obstacles that await me. Please remember that Christianity is not a Sunday practice only, but an everyday lifestyle that consists of daily prayer and studying the Word of God. Lives are changed and masks are taken off when we put in the work.

Being a Christian is who you are, it is not something you pick up and put down whenever you feel like it. Studying your Bible, teaching and preaching are done for your everyday life.

Big Decisions
You can't make decisions based on fear and the possibility of what might happen.
-Michelle Obama-

At the time of this writing, I am twenty-five years old and have faced many crossroads in life already. The decisions we make on a daily bases dictate where we will end up that day, week, month, and in years to come. These decisions determine opportunities you will get, how lives will be changed and what rewards are received.

These decisions can also bring forth bad fruit, lost opportunities and negative outcomes. So, how in the world do you make these big decisions in life? How do you choose what school to attend, what to major in, who to marry, how to spend money, what church to attend and more?

Before any big decision you make I encourage you to remember and believe Romans 8:28: *and we know that all things work together for good to those who love God, to those who are the called according to His purpose.*

In order to get the good stuff out of that verse you have to love God. In John 14:15 it says, *If you love Me, keep My commandments.* Making big decisions are easier when you know your gifts and purpose. I do not have the secret sauce to making big decisions because we each have our own choices to make. I just encourage you to do three things before making these big decisions in life.

Unmask

FIRST

Pray! Jeremiah 33:3 says, *Call on Me and I will answer you and show you great and mighty things that you do not know.* God promises that He will answer us when we pray. Ask God for wisdom to make the correct decision. Look at James 1:5: *If any of you lacks wisdom, let him ask of God, who gives to all liberally and without reproach, and it will be given to him.* God wants you to check with Him through prayer before every decision, *In all your ways acknowledge Him, and He shall direct your paths,* (Proverbs 3:6). Repentance is always important because, *God does not hear the prayer of those who have iniquity in their heart* (Psalm 66:19).

SECOND

Check with the Word of God! You want to make sure that you are not in direct opposition with the Word of God. This will save you a lot of pain and unwanted suffering. Making a big decision that directly goes against the Will of God is dangerous because you are not putting your trust in the Lord. And God will not bless anything that goes against His Word.

THIRD

Get godly council! Big decisions are not to be made alone. Godly council is important because a godly person is not afraid to tell you what you do not want to hear. A godly person will tell you the truth even if it hurts. But at the end of the day the choice is yours. A lot of the proverb Scriptures below deal with getting godly council.
Additional Scriptures to study:

Additional Scriptures to study:

Deuteronomy 28:1-2
Jeremiah 33:3
Psalm 1:1-3, 119:24,
Proverbs 11:14, 15:22, 24:6
Mark 11:24
1 Corinthians 10:31
James 1:5

Commitment:

_____
_____
_____
_____
_____
_____

Friends
If you hang out with chickens, you're going to cluck and if you hang out with eagles, you're going to fly.
-Dr. Steve Maraboli-

Your friends really do matter. Think about the influence your friends have on your life. Friends may have talked you into making wiser choices. You may have talked some of your friends out of making a foolish decision. And some friends may have talked you in to doing some insane things. A friend once convinced me to steal gas from the gas station. I was stealing gas for about two months before one of our friends got caught. I know that is pretty insane.

The Bible has something to say about the friends you keep. I am talking about your inner circle; the ones who you will listen to and share your deepest fears, dreams and decisions. In order to be a Young Courageous Christian it is important that you are careful whom you call your friend.

I am not saying that you drop every person who does not love Jesus the way you do. I am saying, it is easier to pull someone down than up. A friend is all about love. Under the section "Real Love," we find out what real love is (1 Corinthians 13:1-8). Hold your real friends to the real love standard. Make sure you are being the friend that you want someone to be to you!

I separated from friends and their bad habits when they pressured me to a point where I couldn't say no. I use to struggle with saying no to weed, liquor and a whole bunch of stuff because I was not strong enough in my Word. I kept wearing these masks trying to please my friends. When I took off my masks and separated myself from my friends, I got strong enough to say no, but was still able to hang out with them when I chose to.

I soon found out that because of my new lifestyle, they didn't want to be around me. That can be difficult to deal with, but remember God wants the best for you and He will provide friends who will help you grow closer to Him. God has brought a lot of new friends into my life who love Him and want to hold me accountable.

Unmask

Be honest. The friends you may have had in your life since elementary school, your "ride or die" buddies and even family members may be hurting your relationship with God. They encourage you to do sin and make poor choices. Write down their names. Then, write the names of those who really help you obey God and hold you accountable. Make your commitment based on the additional Scriptures to study!

_____

_____

_____

Additional Scriptures to study:

1 Samuel 18:1-5 (David and Jonathan friendship)
Proverbs 12:26, 16:28, 17:9, 17:17, 18:24, 19:4, 27:6, 27:17
Ecclesiastes 4:9-12

Commitment:

_____

_____

_____

_____

_____

_____

Parents
Most parents just want you to avoid the same foolish mistakes they made.
-Mo Brooks-

Believe it or not, your parents (especial godly parents) know what they are talking about. Most parents want their children to be better than themselves and avoid making the same foolish mistakes they made. The Bible says we must honor our parents no matter what they have done.

Children, obey your parents in the Lord, for this is right. Honor your father and mother, which is the first commandment with promise: that it may be well with you and you may live long on the earth.
Ephesians 6:1-3

No one is perfect—not even our parents. It is so important to understand this and to forgive them for any mistakes they have made. There are great promises attached to honoring your parents. It can be tough honoring a parent who has treated you wrongfully or hurt your feelings deeply, but it can be done. In chapter one, you saw the deep wound my father afflicted upon me. But I still forgive him.

I really want to highlight the fact of forgiving the parents who have hurt you. If you have great parents you need to wake up and recognize that. You need to take advantage of the gift God has given you and listen to the abundance of wisdom they are trying to pour into your life. Parents who have abused, misused and mistreated you can be hard to honor. Remember that *all have sinned and fallen short of the glory of God* (Romans 3:23).

It is important to know your family history and why your parents behave the way they do. Is there a spirit of alcoholism in your family? What about a history of abuse? If you know this information you may find it easier to forgive your parents because you understand that is a part of their journey. That does not excuse their actions but it does give you a better understanding. Please do not forget that there is a blessing attached to honoring your parents.

Unmask

Parents make mistakes and most parents really want the best for you. Forgive, love, and honor your parents. Without them you would not be in this world today. So, for that fact alone, honor your parents for this will be good for you.

Additional Scriptures to study:

Exodus 20:12
Deuteronomy 6:7-9
Proverbs 10:1, 19:26, 20:20, 22:6, 28:24
Ephesians 6:1-4, Colossians 3:20-21

Commitment:

_____
_____
_____
_____

Foster Children (Father/Motherless)
It's not where you start – it's where you finish that counts.
-Zig Ziglar-

Most of my teenage years were spent without my father. Some of you have been in the foster care system due to abuse, neglect, imprisonment or the death of your parents. This is a big and tough pill to swallow. How do you fill that void in your heart? All you want is to be loved and feel loved by your parents. You see other families and you are jealous because you want to experience that love and bond they share.

Not having or knowing your parents can have an everlasting impact on your life. It is very beneficial to take advantage of counseling and therapy to help with these emotional and mental holds on your life. I know a God who can heal and deliver from any situation.

I only scratched the surface of this topic, but it will be up to you to dig deeper. God is a father to the fatherless and a mother to the motherless. God will fill that void that is in your heart and He will provide mother and father figures in your life to give you what you need.

When you say God is a provider, you are saying that He will provide EVERYTHING you need. We all need mothers and fathers in our lives. Do not miss the people in your life who care and love you, maybe better than your real parents. Those people are in your life to help fill that void. Do not let what your parents did or did not do to hinder the love someone else is trying to show you!

Unmask:

You may need to go to a pastor or counselor to help you face this huge issue head on. Do not run from it because running will not solve the issue in your heart. God loves you and He will never leave you nor forsake you. Learn to trust again, and know that all people are not out to hurt you. Please read the additional Scriptures and apply them to your life. Read them over and over again. Know that God is there for you and your birth is not a mistake.

Additional Scriptures to study:

Psalm 68:5-6, 139:1-18
Jeremiah 1:5
John 1:12-13
Romans 8:14-15
Ephesians 1:5

Commitment:

_____

_____

_____

_____

_____

_____

Anger
Speak when you are angry and you will make the best speech you will ever regret.
-Ambrose Bierce-

To be angry is a natural emotion. Some find it easy to control anger while others really struggle with it. Take it from me, when you are angry don't talk or make any decisions you will regret.

Scripture shows that the person who is angry is not wise. *Do not hasten in your spirit to be angry, For anger rests in the bosom of fools* (Ecclesiastics 7:9). Do you know why you are so angry? A person who is in a constant state of anger is not really angry at a current situation or person. This person is dealing with the issue of controlling this emotion called anger. If you struggle with anger sit down and recall past events that you have not healed from yet.

Maybe you are angry because a person who was close to you died. Maybe you were betrayed by a close friend. Maybe your father left you at a young age and you do not know why. Do not allow these past situations to control your life. *Jesus came that you have life and life more abundantly* (John 10:10b). Your anger is controlling your life and you need to do something before you do or say something that you will regret.

Unmask

Write down why you think you are so angry. Write down past hurts, disappoints and major pains that you have not healed from. Now, read and apply these Scriptures concerning anger. As you obey the scripture you will find your anger problem being reduced. Also, find another mature Christian to talk to about what you are angry about.

Additional Scriptures to study:

Psalm 37:8
Proverbs 14:17, 29, 15:1, 18, 22:24-25, 29:11
Matthew 5:21-22
Ephesians 4:26-27, 31

Commitment:

_____

_____

Self-esteem
Wanting to be someone else is a waste of the person you are.
-Marilyn Monroe-

God gave us a commandment to *Love your neighbor as you love yourself* (Matthew 22:37). God actually wants you to love yourself. Have confidence in who God created you to be. It is okay to be aware of your weaknesses and insecurities because we all have them. It is not okay *not* to love yourself because of your weaknesses and insecurities. If you do not love yourself then you may not understand what God did when He created you. You may not understand who God is and that He cannot make a mistake. You may not understand that there is only one you and that you are valuable, special and beloved.

Who are you? To be a Young Courageous Christian you must know who you are. God does not make junk. Knowing who you are will unlock godly self-esteem. Now, please do not get carried away with self-esteem because we must be careful anytime we talk about esteeming self. Like and love who you are as a Christian. Remember you are supposed to be different so do not act like someone you are not just to fit in. Do not put on a mask! Remember, an apple cannot be an orange no matter how hard it tries.

Unmask

Believe that you have value, worth and beauty. Speak highly of yourself and do not speak one negative word concerning yourself or others. When others try to put you down through jokes and negative words do not believe them! Reject and do not accept their hurtful words.

People will talk about you just because you are alive, so get accustom to it and do not allow them to get you down. You are who God says you are because His opinion is the only one that matters. Remember, Jesus was talked about too.

If the world hates you, you know that it hated Me before it hated you.
If you were of the world, the world would love its own. Yet because
you are not of the world, but I chose you out of the world,
therefore the world hates you.
John 15:18-19

Additional Scriptures to study:

Genesis 1:26-31
Psalm 139: 13-18
Jeremiah 1: 4-9
Ephesians 1:3-14,
1 Timothy 4:12-16

Commitment:

_____
_____
_____
_____
_____
_____

Suicide
God loves you and you are needed.
-The Truth-

This is a heavy subject and is very important to talk about. I have been trained as a suicide prevention specialist, so I am not talking ignorantly about this subject. I had suicidal thoughts when one or two things had occurred in the past.

At first I felt like my life did not matter. I felt like I had no idea why I was on earth and just got tired of going through the trials of life. Secondly, and more thought provoking, was I felt I was not meeting the high expectations of others.

I felt like I could not meet the goals and expectations they set for me. From coaches, family, girlfriends and God. Each time I failed at something I felt so bad, down and low; especially when it came to finishing my Bachelor's degree. I made myself feel like it was impossible to accomplish.

Listen, you are loved and you are here for a reason. It is okay if you do not know the reason yet. It is okay if you think you do not meet the expectations of others—even God! That is why He has mercy, grace, forgiveness, and longsuffering. So, do not get bent out of shape just because you made a mistake because we all have.

Suicide is the most selfish act a human can make. There is no concern for how it will affect your family, friends, and loved ones. To be honest, you love and care about others as well. So talk to a trusted adult if you are having suicidal thoughts because those thoughts must go! God has a future planned for you even if you cannot see it or understand it just yet. Do not be afraid to seek help. We need you and love you!

Suicide is a negative coping skill. Anyone thinking about suicide is looking for a way to end the emotional, physical, spiritual, mental or social pain they may be going through or have previously experienced. If you or someone you know is thinking about suicide please get help now.

There are many ways to cope with pain in a healthy manner. Maybe you or that other person cannot see those ways now, but those ways are out there. Some of those ways include participating in your favorite hobbies, talking to a friend, writing, getting professional help just to name a few.

Unmask

Are you thinking about suicide? If so, please talk to a trusted adult NOW! The way you kill negative thoughts is through speaking. So speak positive things and seek help. If someone you know had a relationship with Christ and they completed suicide, know that they did not lose their salvation. For once someone is truly born again then they are always saved.

Please check on your friends and make sure they are not having suicidal thoughts, especially when a traumatizing event has happened in their life.

Call 381-HELP or 1 (800) 273-8255 to speak with someone to help you confidentially! This hotline is open 24/7 (even on holidays).

Additional Scriptures to study:

Psalm 139: 13-18
Isaiah 61:10
John 3:16-17, 10:22-30, 15:16,
Philippians 4:4-9

Commitment:

_____
_____
_____
_____

Forgiveness
You can't forgive without loving. And I don't mean sentimentality. I don't mean mush. I mean having enough courage to stand up and say, I forgive. I'm finished with it.
-Maya Angelou-

Forgiveness is a huge struggle for a lot of people—even Christians. Read Matthew 18:21-35. God looks at us as the servant who has been forgiven a great debt but will not forgive another for a small debt! See, it is easy to forgive when you understand the extent you have been forgiven by God.

To say that it is hard to forgive is to say that you do not know how much God forgave you. Do not use the excuse, "You do not understand what they did to me!" You are right. I do not understand. But God does and He demands we forgive others in order to receive His forgiveness.

Unmask

Forgiveness is a command from the God of the universe. Ask God to reveal your own sin that you may forgive others easier. Read these forgiveness Scriptures.

It does not matter what others have done to you, God says forgive other people because He forgave you! The sin that I committed toward God cost so much more than the sin others committed toward us (Matthew 18:21-35). Please read and reread this scripture until you understand it, believe it and walk in it. Tweet me if you have any questions: @mo_brooks or email me: **mobrooksycc@gmail.com.**

Additional Scriptures to study:

Matthew 18:21-35; Matthew 6:14-15
Mark 11:25-26
Galatians 6:1-2
Ephesians 4:29-32

Commitment:

_____
_____
_____
_____
_____

Stewardship

Economics for Everybody begins with understanding God's principles for organizing His creation and what that means for us as creatures and stewards.

-R. C. Sproul-

God owns everything on earth because He created it. *In the beginning God created the heavens and the earth.* (Genesis 1:1). *The earth is the Lord's, and all its fullness, The world and those who dwell therein* (Psalm 24:1). God has given us the earth to be good stewards over it.

There are three major areas you can be a great steward in:

Your resources (money/things),

Your time, and

Your God-given gifts.

If you can grasp this at a young age, you can avoid a lot of unneeded heartaches. God wants us to take care of what He owns. Stewardship goes wrong when you forget that God is the owner. We are to manage and take care of everything that God has placed in our hands.

Have you ever driven someone else's car? How did you drive that car? You probably drove carefully; ensuring that you returned the care in the same shape you received it. When I borrow a car, I put gas in it and even wash it before I return it. God really expects us to do just as much for what He has blessed us with.

Unmask

Are you a good steward when it comes to your resources (money/things), time and your God-given gifts? Are you wasteful and do not take care of things because you think it is yours? Well stewardship takes discipline, which is hard work. When it comes to your money make sure you tithe to your local church, and save for your future. When it comes to your time, do not waste it on foolish things. When it comes to your God-given gifts, work on sharpening those gifts that you may use them to bless someone else.

Additional Scriptures to study:

Malachi 3: 8-12
Luke 12:35-48, 16:1-13
1 Corinthians 8: 1-15

Commitment:

_____
_____
_____
_____

Real Love
Do not get it twisted; love is not lust by any means.
-Mo Brooks-

What is real love? Can I tell you what real love is not? Real love is not pure feeling, emotion and your heart skipping a beat. All of those things may be included in real love but does not speak to what love really is entirely. There are different types of love. Our English language simplifies the word love. We say, "I love my dog," or "I love pizza," and "I love my mother." I am sure you love your mother on a different level than a dog and pizza.

One type of love that most people are familiar with is the type of love God has for us. This is the type of love parents are to have for their children. This is the type of love you want your marriage to be founded, sustained and maintained upon. This love is called agape love, or better known as unconditional love.

Unconditional love means that I love you no matter what you do and who you are. The reason why feelings and emotions are not a heavy part of unconditional love is because this love is a commitment. Relationships will come to a point where someone will get on your nerves or offend you. Real love is what holds relationships together over a long period of time despite these unforeseen emotions. Real love is committed to 1 Corinthians 13:1-8.

Pastor James Harris of Trenches Community Church in Kalamazoo, Michigan, challenged me through one of his lessons. He said, "If you want to know if you are loving someone or not, replace the word love, in 1 Corinthians 13:1-8, with your name e.g. "Mo suffers long and is kind; Mo does not envy..." Do the same thing if you want to see if someone else is loving you or not."

Do not base love on what you see on TV or hear in music, but base it off the Word of God. God is our perfect example of how to love Him and others. Since God is love, every biblical account is showing us how to love Him and others. Since God is love you need Him to love authentically. At the end of the day God gave us two commandments that you should read in Matthew 22:37-40. Remember you cannot love without God working through you by the way of the Holy Spirit.

Unmask

Love check. Are you loving people? Change your definition of love. Love according to scripture, not what society says. If he/she loves you they would be okay waiting until marriage to have sexual relations.

Loves does not try to get others to sin, but has a desire for others to obey God because it is best for them both. I pray that you will be able to see the mask of lust and take it off if you are wearing it.

Additional Scriptures to study:

John 14:15
1 Corinthians 13:1-8
Matthew 22:37-40
John 3:16-17
Romans 5:8-11, 8:31-39
1 John 2:10-11, 3:10-15, 3:16-23, 4:7-11, 4:15- 5:5

Commitment:

_____
_____
_____
_____
_____
_____

Protection

I cannot think of any need in childhood as strong as the need for a father's protection.
-Sigmund Freud-

God is your Father. He loves you and really wants the best for you. God has many promises concerning your protection as His child. The key to God's protection is to stay in His house. Most of you grew up in a home where your food was provided and you had some sort of protection. If you were to leave that house you would open your life up to so many dangers.

A father's arms should be the safest place in the world. If you did not experience a father growing up or your father did not provide that security, do not worry because God said He is a father to the fatherless (Psalm 68:5).

Unmask

The Word of God is your ultimate protection insurance. No matter what happens you are safe. God is your Father!

Additional Scriptures to study:

Psalm 27:1-14, 84:11
Isaiah 54:17
Matthew 28:16-20
2 Corinthians 10:3-6
Luke 15:11-32
Ephesians 6:10-20
Hebrews 13:5

Commitment:

_____
_____
_____
_____
_____
_____

Patience
I am sure God keeps no one waiting unless He sees that it is good for him to wait.
-C.S. Lewis-

Patience is a beautiful virtue! Our generation is called the Microwave Generation because we want everything to happen NOW. Hebrews 10:36 has the perfect scripture for this topic. We are in need of patience and we have to work diligently to make sure we are exercising patience in our lives. Patience is important because God has this thing called timing. If you look throughout the scripture you will find the timing of God always works out. The promises of God may not come to fruition right away and trusting in the timing of God through patience will help you along the way.

I think it is very important to know that God is patient. I cannot say this enough, God will not ask you to do something or be something if He is not that Himself! The patience of God will never run dry. That is a blessing because if God were not patient, that would mean we would be in big trouble!

Unmask

Do you have patience? If not, and you want it, you might not like how you get it. You get patience through trials and temptations, James 1:2-4. So, when traffic is backed up, the grocery store line is packed, sexual temptation is knocking on your door or someone has made you angry, there is opportunity to build and grow your patience. If you want more patience you have to think before you act and know that everything will work out because you trust in Jesus.

Additional Scriptures to study:

Psalm 86:15, Romans 2:6-7, 5:1-5, 8:24-25
Galatians 5:22-26, 1 Timothy 1:16
James 1:2-4, Hebrews 10:26, 2 Peter 3:9

Commitment:

_____

_____

_____

_____

_____

Death/Grieving
If you keep on living someone close to you will die.
-Unknown-

It is nearly impossible to prepare for someone's death. My two beloved grandparents were in hospice care and given less than six months to live. I knew that they did not have that much time left before going to be with our Lord, but the pain and sorrow I felt was just as intense as if they died from sudden death.

Whether you know, or don't know when someone is about to die, it is still a painful experience. How do we handle this pain? What do we need to know about death? Death has no prejudice and does not discriminate. When death happens to someone we love we can feel pain, sorrow, sadness, anger, depression and confusion. These emotions are very normal and expected. There may be a problem if these emotions or feelings last for too long.

I am not saying that you cannot miss your loved one and think about them. I am saying that grieving is a process and that process may be a life-long journey depending on the details of the death. At some point of time that process should not hinder everyday living. God did not design anyone to live in a state of depression, sorrow, sadness, anger or confusion.

Knowing what the Bible says about death can help you get through the grieving process. I look at death differently as a Christian who knows what the Bible says about death. Unless Jesus comes back while you are living, EVERYONE has to die. We cannot avoid death but we can learn how to deal with death in a godly way that will glorify Him.

I want to encourage you not to use the death of your loved one as an excuse to sin. How disrespectful it is to that person and their family if you to get drunk or high in "respect" to that person's memory. I am guilty of this and I am sorry that I did such a thing. My loved ones deserve better than that, and yours do too.

When a loved one dies you can use that as an opportunity to serve, pray for and love your family. Your family needs you during times like these. This is what being a Young Courageous Christian is about; having enough courage to be the Christian God called you to be, even in the mist of hardship, pain and suffering.

Unmask

What is your first reaction when a loved one dies? Please try to make it a habit to run to God when hardships hit you and your family. Pray and cry out to God! You will find a lot of Scriptures that will help you through this process. This is a time period where the Word will benefit you and bless you in ways you cannot imagine.

Additional Scriptures to study:

Psalm 23, 46
John 14:1-6
Romans 8:16-17, 28
1 Corinthians 15:1-58,
2 Corinthians 5:6-8
1 Thessalonians 4:16-18, 5:9-11

Commitment:

_____
_____
_____
_____

Sharing your faith
One thing you cannot do in heaven- share your faith.
-Mark Cahill-

If you had millions of dollars, what are some things you would do with that money? I hope one of those things would be give some away to people who really need it! Which is more valuable to you, millions of dollars or a relationship with Jesus? If you think it is a millions of dollars you may have to check your relationship with Jesus because He is worth far more than riches that cannot get you into heaven.

The person who truly has Jesus in their lives wants to share Him because they understand His true worth! I am afraid of the so-called Christian who does not share their faith with ANYBODY! If you did not know this was a

Christian responsibility, well now you do.

God commands His people to be a witness. The very purpose of the Holy Spirit is to be a witness (Acts 1:8). Who should we share our faith with? According to Matthew 28:16-20, a lot of you may be thinking that you do not know how. It is simple, start off with your own story of how God changed your life. Now tell your story to someone.

I believe that a lot of young people do not feel conformable sharing their faith because of the lifestyle they are living. You say, "I do not want to be a hypocrite." That is an issue because what you are really saying is, "I am not living for Christ like I ought to therefore I refuse to share my faith." You feel you cannot consistently post and tweet about Jesus because deep down inside you know you are not trying to live for Jesus in all areas of your life.

Unmask

Take off that mask that is covering up your Christianity! Stop trying to blend in with the crowd at the expense of covering up your faith. God called you to be a witness of His salvation that someone else may be saved. Your family, friends and strangers need Jesus or their eternal life is in danger. Write down 5 people you can share your faith with. Those five people can be strangers, friends or family members. Pray and step out on faith and you will find out that it was not as hard as you imagine.

Additional Scriptures to study:

Matthew 5:14-16, 9:35-38, 28:16-20
Mark 16:14-18
Acts 1:8,
2 Corinthians 5:12-21
1 Timothy 2:1-7
2 Peter 2:9

Commitment:

_____
_____
_____
_____

Discipleship
No discipleship leads to isolation, lack of accountability and loss of faith.
-Mo Brooks-

What happens if you are sharing your faith and someone says, "Yes, I am ready to give my life to Christ?" Attached to sharing your faith comes the responsibility of discipleship. Please do not let this term frighten you. Discipleship can be summed up as, teaching someone else how to follow Jesus.

How did you learn how to tie your shoes? How did you learn your ABC's? How did you learn what a Zebra is? Someone who already knew taught you. The Christian has the responsibility of not only sharing their faith but teaching others how to be a Christian in their everyday life.

If God helped you stopped cussing, now it is your responsibility to help someone else do the same. Who is teaching you? Who is showing you how to apply the Word of God in your life? Who do you go to when you have questions about the faith or life? Who holds you accountable to ensure you are repenting from sin and staying away from your old sinful habits? Some of you might be struggling with answering these questions.

If you cannot connect a name with these questions then you need to find someone who is willing to disciple you. Yes, your parents should be doing this but if that is not the case someone in your church will be willing if you ask. As you help someone else in the faith and hold them accountable, it will benefit you. That person will challenge you and push you in ways that you would not expect. So, get ready to grow as you help another with their walk.

Unmask

If you do not have a person who is holding you accountable and showing you how to live for Christ seek them out. Find that person. Find someone who will allow you to help them with their walk in Christ. Remember it is a two-way street because as you help them, you will quickly find out that they are helping you grow just as much.

Additional Scriptures to study:

**Proverbs 27:17, Matthew 28:19,
Mark 1:16-22 1 Corinthians 11:1,
2 Timothy 2:1-3**

Commitment:

Advice
Why take advice from a fool?
-Mo Brooks-

Who does the most talking in a classroom? The teacher. They are the experts of that particular subject. What sense does it make to go to a person who does not know more than you for advice or help? Crazy, but a lot of us go to our friends who have little experience concerning life. Where do you go to get advice? Before you make decision and you want someone else's opinion, think of whom you will go to?

Be smarter! Go to someone who is wise, had success and has advice based on Scripture. Stop going to your like-minded friends for these life-altering decisions to justify a decision you know is wrong. Of course your young horny friend is going to tell you to have sex! Go to someone who will tell you what you may not want to hear, but it is for your own good.

Unmask

Evaluate who you go to when you need advice or are dealing with problems. Write those names down. After you have written those names, cross out those who you know are not giving you godly advice!

Additional Scriptures to study:

Psalm 1:1-3

Commitment:

Boredom
Boredom (an idle mind) is the Devil's playground.
-Anonymous-

When it comes to being bored the Bible calls that an idle mind. For a mind to be idle is not a hard thing. The reason for any source of entertainment is help your mind get into a state of idleness. During a trip to the movies, before the movie began, an advertisement message said, "Please enjoy your break from reality." I could not focus on the movie because my mind was on how this movie was going to give me a "break" from reality. I then began to wonder, what else is designed to give me a break from reality?

See, my reality is the presence of God, my family, purpose, goals and so forth. How many breaks do I take from reality on a daily bases? How many breaks do you take from reality? Being bored is not fun. Being bored is birthed out of a lack of purpose and goals to accomplish. If I find myself bored, I find it a sin to be idle. I could be studying, praying, sharing my faith, resting, spending time with family and people I love.

When we are bored the devil seems to have fun because he will try to fill up our mind with sinful ideas. You may want to call that girl or boy you have no business of calling. You find yourself wasting valuable time with that idol (TV, video games, gossip, etc.) that takes you away from God.

The cure for boredom is purpose. When you know why you were born it creates direction for what you need to be doing at any given time. Time is the one thing on earth we cannot get back. Once time is spent, it is gone. The key indicator that you are bored is that you are trying to fill up your day with things that entertain you.

Please do not get me twisted! I am all for rest, rejuvenation and fun. My focus here is boredom that leads to laziness and idleness that leads to sin. One of my favorite scriptures in the Bible that helps me set my limits with rest and entertainment is Proverbs 25:16: *Have you found honey? Eat only as much as you need, lest you be filled with it and vomit.*

Unmask

What do you do when you are bored? The key to combat boredom is by working on your purpose. If you do not know your purpose, work on finding it. Track how you spend your time. If you list things that hinder your relationship with Christ, cut them out. There are plenty of godly things to do like spend time with your family, work on your goal, or clean your home.

Additional Scriptures to study:

Nehemiah 2:17-18
Proverbs 19:15
Ecclesiastes 10:18
Ephesians 2:10, 5:14-17
Philippians 4:8
2 Timothy 2:16

Commitment:

_____
_____
_____
_____
_____
_____
_____

Integrity and Character
A good character is the best tombstone.
-Charles Spurgeon-

In chapter one I talked about behaving two different ways based on who you are around. That entire chapter speaks to integrity and character. Integrity and character is how you behave when no one is looking. In the Christian realm it means—in its simplest form— can you obey God even when no one is looking? Can you remain a disciple when no one is pushing you to? Can you be honest when no one knows the truth except for you? Can you be honest, even though it seems that lying will benefit you more?

As a Christian, leader, family member, employer, employee or any other role we hold in this society, integrity and character is the number-one characteristic needed. It means you are trustworthy and are able to handle more responsibility. Your gifts, talents and passion can help you do anything God has created you to do, but if integrity and character are absent you will ruin everything that God has blessed you with. More importantly, you will not glorify the Lord.

Unmask

Be who you say you are, all the time! If you say you are a Christian be one 24/7! If you say you are a student, study. If you say you are son/daughter respect and check on your parents. The list can go on and on. Whoever you are live that out every day and be consent. Do not change just because you think you can get away with something when no one is looking. If you cannot do it in public you probably should not be doing it behind closed doors. Better yet, if you cannot do it in front of Jesus, don't do it!

Additional Scriptures to study:

Genesis 39:1-15
Job 2:9-10, 21:6, 27:5
Psalm 7:8, 25:21, 26:11, 41:12
Proverbs 10:9, 11:3, 20:7, 28:6
Matthew 5:37, 7:15-20, Luke 8:17,
Titus 2:7
1 Peter 1:16

Commitment:
_____
_____
_____

Leadership
Do not apologize for being a leader.
-Unknown-

It is easy to follow. You do not need a lot of courage to follow. Leadership not only takes courage but leaders learn not to be afraid to make mistakes or be embarrassed. We wear those masks of a follower because we think living for Christ will cause us to be embarrassed. Leaders are not afraid of what others think.

Leadership calls for you to be a person of integrity and character. It calls for being two steps ahead of those who are following you. Having a position or title does not make you a leader. Leadership is earned through building relationships, being faithful and getting results. Also, being a great follower of a great leader will help you become a great leader.

Leadership is not to be taken lightly. Most of the problems that exist in the church and the world are due to poor, or the lack of leadership. One of the hardest things I had to experience as a leader was taking responsibility for someone else's mistake. When you are a leader and anything goes wrong, you have to take responsibility. Following Jesus will cultivate your leadership. Remember, you are not a leading if there is no body following you (John Maxwell).

Unmask

As a Christian you will have to lead someone to Christ, lead someone to a closer relationship with Christ or stand up for what you believe. You will not be able to follow the crowd. Who are you leading in the right direction? Are the people around you growing closer to Christ because of your leadership? Take off that mask of a follower and step up to be the leader God called you to be.

Additional Scriptures to study:

Story of Moses (Exodus)
Story of Gideon (Judges 6-8)
Story of Daniel (Daniel)
Story of Jesus (Matthew-John)
1 Corinthians 11:1
Galatians 1:10

Commitment:

_____
_____
_____
_____
_____

The Book of Proverbs
For precept must be upon precept, precept upon precept, Line upon line, line upon line, Here a little, there a little.
-Isaiah 28:10-

One of the biggest problems I faced when trying to help young people study their Bible on their own is showing them where to start. Proverbs is a great book to read when starting to read the Bible. It is full of directions and principles to apply to your life right away. One Proverb a day can really help build the habit of reading God's Word every day!

Unmask

If you are having trouble on where to start reading your Bible, read a Proverb a day and continue working through this book! Remember to apply/obey/do the Word that you read.

Additional Scriptures to study:

Proverbs chapters 1-31

Commitment:

_____
_____
_____
_____
_____
_____

Part 4

UNMASKing
Temptation

Temptation is everywhere but God has given us everything we need to defeat this defeated foe.

Overcoming Temptation

Temptation is one of the biggest excuses used by Christians and non-Christians when it comes to not living for Jesus. In this part, I want to unmask temptation for what it really is. I want to expose a lot of common temptations you face as a Young Courageous Christian and what you will be facing for the rest of your life.

Jesus died to disarm the principalities and powers of the enemy and to destroy the works of the devil (Colossians 2:15 and 1 John 3:8). Jesus died so you can have dominion over sin. Jesus showed us how to defeat temptation on earth as a human. All throughout scripture you will find instructions to follow effectively to overcome temptation. Jesus is our perfect Example!

Please know that giving in to temptation is a trick of the enemy. I once did a radical illustration in my Fulfillment Hour class to make this point. I stood in front of my ninth and tenth graders and asked, "Who wants $35?" Of course all hands went up.

Then I went on to ask, "Who is willing to be brave and volunteer to receive this $35?" Again, all hands went up. I wrote on the board an S, B, F, and H and told them that in order to get the money they would have to say four curse words, one which started with each letter.

The hands of all but four students went down. So, four people said the curse words in front of the class. I went on to say, "These four people were willing to sin for $8.75. They were willing to sin against God in front of God's people all because they wanted to fulfill an evil desire within them." Then I ripped the $35 into pieces saying, "This is what happens when we fall for temptation."

All that glitters is not gold; all is not good that tastes sweet; and all is not real pleasure that pleases for a time. Temptation always looks good, feels good and tastes good. That temptation will always lie to you and leave you in pieces.

Was cursing really worth it? No. The same temptation that seems great will always yield the fruit of pain, heartache, sadness, depression and more negative consequences. *For the wages of sin is death, but the gift of God is eternal life* (Romans 3:23).

If you are a parent, teacher, adult or student offended by the example I used above, realize that most of our young people use filthy language when you are not around. You may not know that because they are wearing a mask to cover it up.

Look in the Mirror
You better check yourself before you wreck yourself.
-Ice Cube-

When it comes to temptation the devil gets all the credit for messing up lives. Yes, the devil is real and he is out to steal, kill and destroy. What if I told you that the devil is not your number-one enemy? Your number-one enemy is the person in the mirror! Until you build the discipline to live a godly life and have some success in Jesus you are your number-one enemy. We have this thing called the flesh, our human bodies. We can never be perfect because of our flesh, which desires everything opposite of the spirit (Galatians 5:16-18). That does not mean that we cannot live godly lives. It means that we have to allow God to rule and direct our lives. The only way this can happen is through growing in the knowledge of God (1 Peter 1:2-4), disciplining our bodies (1 Corinthians 9:27) and denying ourselves/flesh daily (Luke 9:23).

You hear a lot of people say, "the devil is on me." Could it be, that the devil has not done nearly as much as you give him credit for? You have the power to make a choice (Deuteronomy 30:19). Look in the mirror and check to make sure the choices you make are not causing more harm than the devil could.

Lastly, we have to be careful not to put ourselves in the position to sin. Sexual sin is running rampant in our culture today. It is not wise to go over to the house of a person of the opposite sex alone to watch a movie...at night! If you want to spend time with someone you like there are better ways to do that without putting yourself in a position to sin.

Unmask

Let's keep it real. There are a lot of temptations that can be avoided by choosing wiser places and people to hang out with. The additional scriptures are going to challenge you to look at yourself and take action when it comes the temptation that comes from within. Stop blaming the devil for every negative thing that happens in your life and reflect upon your past decisions. Make sure that you are not reaping what you sowed!

Additional Scriptures to study:

Matthew 5:29-30, 7:1-5

Galatians 6:1-3
James 1:12-16 & 21-25
1 Peter 5:5-10

Commitment:

_____
_____
_____
_____
_____

The Devil
Your most dangerous enemy is the one you are unaware of.
-Mo Brooks-

Do you know what a scouting report is? A scouting report is designed to learn about the habits and traits of your enemy so you can be prepared and counter most of their moves. A scouting report gives you an edge over your opponent and helps you defeat them. I want to give you a scouting report on the devil.

Once you know the enemy's tendencies you will be able to recognize, counter and defeat him. Here are a few things you must know about the devil. (You will find the scouting report in the additional scriptures section.)

* Know the devil's history. You may have heard already but the devil was an angel in heaven. He was kicked out of heaven because he wanted to be God. Satan and his demons were sentenced to hell for eternal life. From heaven he was sent to earth and his number-one mission has been to steal, kill and destroy mankind's chances of everlasting life with God.

* Know Satan is the father of all lies. He created the lie and hates people. He wants as many as possible to join him in a hell that was not created for people.

* Know Satan is a spirit. He lives in our disobedience. He cannot have free reign over your life. If he had that power, we would all be dead. Satan has some power, but not *all* power.

* Know that the voice of Satan will always go directly against the Word of God. That is why it is so important to know your Word so you can know the Father's voice. Satan is only as powerful as you allow him to be. As a Christian you have the authority to resist him steadfast in the faith.

* Know that Satan is a defeated foe! God has cursed him in Genesis 3. Jesus whooped Him in Matthew chapter 4. The biggest blow was when our Lord Jesus the Christ died on the cross for our sin, was buried and resurrected with all power in His hand!

The gospel of Jesus made a public spectacle of the devil (Colossians 2:15). So, know that your enemy cannot harm you unless God allows him too. If God allows him to do anything, it is always for your good, even when you cannot understand it.

Unmask

I gave you a short scouting report on the devil himself. It is now up to you to read the additional Scriptures and apply every God-given instruction to your daily life. Satan wants to stop you from being saved and once salvation has taken place he wants to kill your witness. Do not allow him to do neither because you are a Young Courageous Christian.

Additional Scriptures to study:

*Genesis 3:1-1-24, Job 1:6-12, 2:1-7, Isaiah 14:12-15
John 8:37-47, 10:10, 2 Corinthians 4:4, Ephesians 6:11-18
1 Peter 5:8, Revelation 12:9-10, 20:10*

Commitment:

_____
_____
_____
_____
_____
_____

I just keep sinning
Do not use your sin as an excuse to keep sinning but use your
sin as an excuse to repent.
-Mo Brooks-

Everyone will agree that they are not perfect and they have room for growth. We call this process sanctification. Sanctification says as long as we are in the flesh (living on earth) there is room to improve our Christ-likeness. Sanctification is when our actual lives are transformed through the Holy Spirit to be more like Christ. A lot of times we Christians cry over spilled milk and never get a towel to clean up the mess. This sanctification comes from repentance from the sin that we are aware of. Trust me, the closer you get to Jesus the more He will show you the sin in your life.

To repent means to change your thinking and to turn away from sin and turn to Jesus. Repenting is not just asking God to forgive you. If you are truly sorry for your sin you will make up your mind to kill that sin through obeying the Word of God. You will seek an accountability partner to assist you in abstaining from that sin. Do not forget that Jesus died for your ability to repent and deliver you from any sin that is hindering you.

Unmask

Do not beat yourself up over your sin (Romans 8:1). Repent and repent fast! Read the first two summaries of Part III to assist you with this process. To stop sinning you must declare war on your sin and get angry at it. Keep praying, studying and hearing the Word of God until you HATE your sin!

Additional Scriptures to study:

2 Chronicles 7:14, Psalms 32:5, 51:1-19, Isaiah 55:6-7
Mark 1:15, Luke 13:1-5, Acts 2:38, 3:19, 17:30-31
Romans 2:4, 2 Peter 3:9, 1 John 1:9

Commitment:

_____
_____
_____
_____

Lust

Do not love the world or the things in the world. If anyone loves the world, the love of the Father is not in him. For all that is in the world—the lust of the flesh, the lust of the eyes, and the pride of life—is not of the Father but is of the world. And the world is passing away, and the lust of it; but he who does the will of God abides forever.

1 John 2:15-16

-God-

Lust is all about wanting what is off limits. The big issue is not the mere fact of wanting something. Some of you are thinking, "Dang we can't want stuff?" No, you can want "stuff," but if you have to jump outside of the boundaries of God to get it, then you have entered the lust category.

Have you ever thought of why God gave us commandments? Why is God so serious about us following His commandments? God is serious about us keeping His commandments because He is trying to protect us from consequences that we cannot see because we are so blinded by our lust. God wants to protect you and at the same time, lust is trying to destroy you. Lust is a self-problem that needs to be exposed.

Do not blame lust on the girls wearing leggings and revealing clothes. Do not blame lust on movies, music and television shows. Lust is a heart problem that can only be solved through prayer and obeying the Word. Please do not mistake lust for love.

Lust is a counterfeit love. Lust looks good, smells good, sounds good and most defiantly feels good. Lust is a trap and will show no mercy once you are entangled in its web. Lust is temporary and will never last forever. Lust starts off with an ecstasy and a pleasure that feels so good but the more you indulge in that lustful sin, the worst it gets.

Lust is a deadly hunter and will chase you for the rest of your life. You cannot fight lust but you have to RUN. 2 Timothy 2:22 says, "Flee also youthful lusts; but pursue righteousness, faith, love, peace with those who call on the Lord out of a pure heart." You will lose every time you try to stand toe-to-toe with lust. I do not care how long you been save or how strong you think you are. If you try to fight lust you will lose. So, run out of the room, turn your head, turn of the television and do whatever you have to do, to run from lust.

As Christians, we put on this mask of strength over lust. We must take that mask off and realize we are WEAK! The quicker we come to this vital truth the quicker we can handle the lust issue in our lives.

Unmask

Be real. What are you lusting after? There is a time to have sex (within marriage). God will meet your needs and desires if you allow Him to. Write down the things you lust after. Talk with a trusted Christian about them. Pray, study and obey the Word and continue to walk with other believers as you run from lust. Remember, you are weak.

Additional Scriptures to study:

Genesis 3:6, 39:6-9, Judges 14-16 (chapters), Job 31:1, Psalms 101:3, Proverbs 5:1-23, 6:20-35, Matthew 5:27-30, 2 Corinthians 12:7-10, 1 Thessalonians 4:1-8, 2 Timothy 2:22, 1 John 2:15-16

Commitment:

_____

_____

_____

_____

_____

Watch your Mouth
Life and death is in the power of the tongue.
Proverbs 18:21

What you say carries weight. Words are powerful and they can hurt or heal. When it comes to being a Young Courageous Christian you have to believe that you can do it! So, what comes out of your mouth as it pertains to your faith? Do you say this is too hard? I cannot do it. I am too young. This is too confusing and too much for me right now. Little do you know, when you constantly say those statements you make them happen.

God has established that there is power in words. After all, He established the world with His words (Genesis 1, Psalm 33:8-9, Hebrews 11:3). God has made you in His image and likeness (Genesis 1:26-27) therefore the words you speak have power. Please watch your mouth in every area of your life. Display integrity and character by speaking godly and positive things even when nobody is around.

Have enough courage to stop using profanity. You may go to school or live with people who curse. But, by not doing the same it will allow your light shine. Some of our language is associated with the music we listen to and the movies we watch. Whatever is in us will come out. So, take of the mask of using profanity because everyone else is using it.

Unmask

As a believer God wants you to speak positive and uplifting things concerning your faith. You believe in Jesus and you want follow Him. Allow your words to line up with your desires. What you say matters and can change your life. I am not talking about "name it and claim it" either. I am talking about obeying Scripture.

Look at the additional Scriptures that show you how God tells us to watch our mouths.

Additional Scriptures to study:

Job 6:24, 20:4, Psalm 12:2-4, 34:13, Proverbs 18:21,
Ephesians 4:29, James 3:1-12

Commitment:

_____
_____
_____
_____
_____
_____

Entertainment
Enjoy your break from reality.
-Celebration Cinema Movie Theater-

I usually get a bad response on this subject because we love entertainment. But I ask, do you grow closer to God by watching movies, sporting events, television series and reality television shows? Are you benefitting because you are watching these things? If your answer is an absolutely yes, then you may struggle with this section.

I am not saying that you cannot watch anything on television or at the movies. I want you to be aware that entertainment takes up a lot of our time as a society and if you get sucked into it, your relationship with God will be weakened.

Entertainment is a deadly trap and can lead to temptations because it can distract you from Jesus and what He wants for your life. Entertainment can eat up all of your time day after day. It can have you pushing your spiritual snooze button over and over again. It can lead to the worship of people, sports teams and celebrities more than Jesus. Being a Young Courageous Christian is a hard thing to live out when feeding ourselves junk.

If you are working to stop using profanity, how in the world are you going to stop when you hang out with friends who use the language? When you watch movies that use foul language and listen to music filled with words you wouldn't say in front of your grandmother? Entertainment has its place but it should by no means supersede our time spent with the Savior through worship, prayer and learning more through His Word.

Unmask

Can you spend more time with Christ and less time with your television, movies, and video games? If yes, make your commitment below. Remember I am not saying that watching movies is a sin but I am saying entertainment can become an idol and lead to wearing more and more masks.

Additional Scriptures to study:

Exodus 20:3, Psalm 101:3, Matthew 10:39, Luke 14:25-26, 1Corinthians 10:31, Philippians 4:8, 1 John 5:21

Commitment:

_____
_____
_____
_____
_____

Lying
Lying can never save us from another lie.
-Vaclav Havel-

Why do you lie? Lying is an ugly habit and will destroy relationships. I think lies are told to keep up with whatever mask you are wearing at the time. Think about it, if you had nothing to hide you would not have a reason to lie. Wearing a mask can lead to producing lies that carry consequences. Why does God hate lying? I believe it is the ultimate mask worn to cover up who we really are.

My mother always told me that she would rather me tell the truth and it crush her, than me tell a lie to make her feel good. My grandmother told me once you tell one lie you have to tell another lie to cover up the first one. This process continues until you forget the first lie you told and get caught up in your own web of deceit. You want to be told the truth, so tell the truth to others. Being a liar is not okay, especially for the Christian.

Every time you lie to someone, you are acting just like the Devil. Think about that. When you lie, you are saying I am behaving like the Devil himself. Where is your heart? Are you courageous enough to tell the truth even when it hurts you or someone else? Being a Christian means to follow Christ—His teachings and his love for the world. Lying is the direct opposite of being Christ-like.

Unmask

Think about the lies you have told over the years. Think about the people you have lied to. Did you really have to lie? Was that lie worth losing the relationship? Put an end to lying today. This temptation is overcome by making a commitment to pleasing God and having the courage to apply it you your life. I beg you to take off your masks and experience the freedom God has in His truth.

Read what God has to say about lying and how seriously He takes it. Just to let you know, the Devil is the father of all lies (John 8:44).

Additional Scriptures to study:

Numbers 23:19, Psalm 119:29, 163, Proverbs 6:17, 12:19, 22, 13:5, 14:5, 25, 19:5, 9, 21:6, John 8:31-36, Acts 5:1-11, Ephesians 4:25

Commitment:

_____

_____

_____

_____

Popularity

For do I now persuade men, or God? Or do I seek to please men? For if I still pleased men, I would not be a bondservant of Christ.
-Apostle Paul-

Everyone wants to be accepted and loved. Most of us want to be popular and that is okay. Being popular is not a bad thing. But putting on different masks to be popular is not okay. What have you done to stay popular? Most young people do everything and will put on any mask to become and stay popular. The clothes, hairstyles, language, relationships—all is built on what other people may think about you. These choices have nothing to do with pleasing God and keeping His commandments.

There's nothing wrong with dressing nicely and having lots of friends but it is all about *why* you are doing those things. Are you trying to be "cool" or are you trying to please God? As a Young Courageous Christian pleasing God is the number-one objective! Chasing popularity will have you doing things to impress people at the expense of sinning against God.

Jesus was popular not because He sought it, but He chose to be Himself. Be yourself (in Christ) and the first sentence of this summary will be yours without compromising your faith. Being a Christian will not always produce popularity. To be honest, in most cases it will do the opposite. When you stand as a Christian you will be talked about, excluded from worldly activities, rejected by people and deemed not cool. To be Christian is to be different than the world, however, God will put the correct people in your life at the right time to meet your social needs.

Unmask

Do you chase popularity? Write down the people you try to impress. Do not say nobody! I know I use to try to impress a lot of my friends. I have to keep guard today from trying to be popular. Make it your personal goal to please God and God alone because you cannot please God and people (Galatians 1:10).

Additional Scriptures to study:

Psalm 118:8, 146:3, Luke 9:23-26, John 15:18-25, Galatians 1:10,
1 Timothy 4:12-16, 2 Timothy 3:12

Commitment:

_____

_____

_____

_____

Love of Money
But those who desire to be rich fall into temptation and a snare, and
intomany foolish and harmful lusts which drown men in
destruction and perdition.
-Apostle Paul-

*Before you start this section please read 1 Timothy 6:9-10

But those who desire to be rich fall into temptation and a snare, and into many foolish and harmful lusts, which drown men in destruction and perdition. For the love of money is a root of all kinds of evil, for which some have strayed from the faith in their greediness, and pierced themselves through with many sorrows.

I do not know about you but this verse is heavy and convicting. A lot of people get it twisted because they think money is evil. Scripture declares the love of money is the root of all kinds of evil (1 Timothy 6:10).

Please understand that money is not good or evil. You have to have the ability to make a choice, for it to be good or evil. Money does not have the ability to make a choice therefore money cannot be good or evil. So, having a lot of money does not make a person good or evil. Having little or no money does not make a person good or evil either. Just because you have a small amount of money does not mean you are cursed with a cursed.

Money is a tool just like a hammer. The hammer is not good or evil. If you put the hammer in the hands of a good person, they will use the hammer to nail nails in their proper place. If you put the hammer in the hands of an evil person, they will use the hammer to bash someone's head in. Likewise, a good person will use money in a godly way and an evil person will use money in an evil way. So, the evil way of using money is through having a love of money over God. Our culture has taught us to depend on money for everything. It has taught us that you are nothing without it.

You have to choose who are you going to serve, God or money. Depend on God not money. Chase after God so you may be a good person through the power of the Holy Spirit, and use money in a way that is pleasing to Him.

Unmask

Do not get sucked into the false security that our culture tries to display. All of your needs and security can be found in Jesus. Check out the additional Scriptures and look at the promises of God and the dangers of loving money. Which one will you choose, God or money?

Additional Scriptures to study:

Psalm 23:1, Matthew 6:19-21, 33, Luke 12:15, 1 Timothy 6:6-10

Commitment:

_____

_____

_____

_____

Sex and Sexual Acts
Flee sexual immorality. Every sin that a man does is outside the body, but he who commits sexual immorality sins against his own body.
1 Corinthians 6:18-

This is probably the most dangerous temptation on earth right now. This temptation has killed many dreams, destinies and futures. It has destroyed families, careers and lives. With knowing all of this information and seeing the damage it has done to a lot of teenagers and adults, sexual sin is still a huge problem. Remember God is not trying to ruin your fun but He desires to protect you.

When you commit sexual sin you learn how to lie, manipulate and deceive. Sexual impurity opens the door to so many others sins outside of sex. Our culture is money and sexual driven. In order to overcome this temptation it will take complete trust in God and His Word. I am currently abstaining from all sexual activity until I am married and I am telling from my own experience that the only thing keeping me from committing any sexual sin is the Word of God, prayer, and accountability.

Unmask

I want to outline some key points on how to abstain from all sexual activity.

* Write down every Scripture that pertains to sexual immorality.

* Work hard on memorizing the scripture (not to show off but to apply in the mist of temptations; Psalm 119:11).

* Do not put yourself in a position to commit sexual sin e.g. going over someone else house late night all by yourself.

* Have 2-4 accountability partners and be open and honest about your struggles, mistakes and victories.

* Stop lusting and looking at sexual images.

* Pray!!! Ask God for help, wisdom, power and strength every day.

Yes, it takes all of this to combat this sin. No, it is not easy but it is worth it. Do not let this sin take you out. I do not care who you are, if you are reading this book, sexual sin will knock at your door. Will you be ready to slam the door in its face?

Additional Scriptures to study:

Matthew 5:27-30, Romans 1:18-32, 1 Corinthians 6:12-20, Galatians 5:16-21, 1 Thessalonians 4:1-8, Hebrews 13:4, Jude 7, Revelation 21:8

Commitment:

_____

_____

_____

_____

Beer and Liquor
What is your purpose of drinking strong drink?
-Mo Brooks-

Is drinking a sin? Can you drink if you do not promise not to get drunk? These are two questions that are heavily debated within the Christian world. I am going to tell you how I approach these two questions and I will strongly encourage you as a Young Courageous Christian.

What is the purpose and motive of drinking an alcohol beverage? Are you thirsty? Do you want something that taste good? Is it because everyone else at the party or club is drinking? Is it your 21st birthday and you want to celebrate you being able to drink according to the law?

People say they drink not to get drunk but to relax and relive stress. Again, I can name plenty of activities and/or hobbies that can help you relax and relive stress. So, why drink? I think the hidden purpose, whether admitted or not, is to get drunk. That desire to have no control and let loose is the real purpose of drinking.

I use to drink to get drunk and I know that I cannot handle it. Also, as a minister of the Gospel of Jesus Christ, 1Timothy 3 commands me not to drink. Beyond those reasons I have a no tolerance for drinking in my life because I want to protect my witness for Jesus and protect my relationship with Jesus. I know that I can fall at any moment so I want to take every precaution to ensure that I do not fall in the trap of drinking alcohol.

I encourage you not to drink alcohol for the simple fact that it has the ability to destroy you and your family. There are more effective ways to handle stress (Philippians 4:4-8), your taste bugs and to celebrate your 21st birthday!

Getting drunk causes you to do things that you normally would not do. Drinking not to get drunk will eventually lead to drinking to get drunk given the right circumstances. The additional Scriptures will support this section and I encourage you to read them and take them serious.

Unmask

If you drink alcohol, why do you drink? Please write that down. It takes courage not to conform to the world and drink. What does Scripture say? In the days of Jesus wine was a lot healthier than water. Also, wine was not loaded down with alcohol like it is now. You had to drink a lot of wine to get drunk in those days. I wanted to make that clear because a lot people try to use that as an excuse to drink but not get drunk. If you are under the age of 21, follow the law and don't drink.

Additional Scriptures to study:

Isaiah 5:11, Habakkuk 2:15-16, Proverbs 20:1, 23:20-21, 31-32, 31:4-7, Romans 14:21, Galatians 5:21, Ephesians 5:18,

Commitment:

_____

_____

_____

_____

_____

Smoking Marijuana
It is impossible to live a surrender life unto God and smoke weed.
-Mo Brooks-

This is a huge epidemic in our country today, especially for young people starting at an alarmingly young age. Smoking marijuana/weed/pot or whatever you call it, is accepted in our culture (for medicinal purposes of course) and is in the process of becoming legalized in several states. What does this information have to do with being a Young Courageous Christian?

If you smoke weed, I beg you to stop! If you have not tired it, I beg you not to! I believe that this drug is one of the sneakiest attacks from Satan himself. I believe that wearing this mask has hinder numerous of people and their relationship with God.

I have experience firsthand how smoking weed has hindered my hearing from God, altered my decision making, lead me to more sin, opened me up to demonic spirits and almost destroyed my life (please read chapter one for more details).

Just like every temptation we have to ask, why do the sin? What does it do for you? Where does it get you? There are healthier ways to relief stress. A lot of people think there is nothing wrong with smoking at all. I really challenge them to have a serious look at their relationship with God.

Can you honestly say that our perfect and holy God is okay with you smoking weed? Can you honestly say you would be okay with a pastor who smoked weed? Could you say that you would be okay with smoking weed in the presence of God? I do not know about you but my answer is a big fat NO to all of those questions.

Just be honest. If you smoke weed, you want to and by now you probably like it. You are probably addicted to smoking. Most people try to justify their sin and bad habits. I am here to challenge you to take off that mask. You probably did not want to start smoking in the first place but someone put that peer pressure on you and you caved.

I promise you that if you stop smoking weed, allow the Word of God to get into you through studying, preaching, teaching and obeying you will experienced God like never before. You will hear God and make better decisions. Obey God and open up to feel the conviction of God that causes repentance.

Unmask

If you do not smoke, don't even think about it. Those who do, it will take courage to take of this mask because your friends who get high will really try to push you to keep smoking. You will have to separate yourself from your smoking friends for a season until you are strong enough to be around them without smoking.

Find a friend who does not smoke, who is going to encourage you every day not to hit the blunt. Most importantly you need a burning desire to quit. God has given every human the power to make choices. This is called free will. If you do not want to stop, nobody can help you.

Additional Scriptures to study:

1 Corinthians 10:31, 1 Peter 1:16

Commitment:

_____
_____
_____
_____

Please visit this website:
www.drugfreeworld.org/drugfacts/marijuana/the-harmful-effects.html

Part 5

UNMASKing
Church and Doctrine

For many deceivers have gone out into the world who do not confess Jesus Christ as coming in the flesh. This is a deceiver and an antichrist. Look to yourselves, that we do not lose those things we worked for, but that we may receive a full reward. Whoever transgresses and does not abide in the doctrine of Christ does not have God. He who abides in the doctrine of Christ has both the Father and the Son. If anyone comes to you and does not bring this doctrine, do not receive him into your house nor greet him; for he who greets him shares in his evil deeds.

2 John 7-11

The Gospel

God is Good and Just! Good is self-existing. Just indicates that God is fair and He must dish out the consequences based on previous choices whether it is a good consequence or bad.

Write down the name of your best friend:

_____

Now, for this illustration, let's say you killed that friend for whatever reason. Your act was caught on surveillance cameras and because you were caught red-handed you pleaded guilty. At your hearing the judge tells you to stand for your sentence.

You stand. The judge says, "You know what? I am feeling like a good judge today. I am also feeling kind, merciful and gracious today. So, today I deem you innocent of the murder of your best friend! Case dismissed."

Is the judge good or bad? You may be happy you got off the hook but whether it is you, someone else or me, letting a murderer go without punishment is flat out wrong and even *you* would want justice for your best friend. Do you agree with that?

Well, we serve a God who is good and just. He is a good judge and the judge who does punish all sin. Romans 3:23 states, *for all have sinned and fall short of the glory of God*. This means that you and I have sinned against God at some point and time in our lives. Yes, God loves us but He has to punish sin because of WHO HE IS! This is why Jesus Christ is a big deal.

Take that same scenario (you killing your best friend) but replace the horrible judge with a good judge. Now, you know this judge's track record and the record states that he does not take his position lightly. This judge stands you up to punish you but just before the word guilty comes out of his mouth Someone interrupts the sentencing.

This Someone says, "Wait! I will take the punishment. Whatever sentence you dish out I will take that." The judge points to the man who interrupts the sentencing and says to him, "As you wish. You are guilty of the crime. I sentence You to death!"

Now the judge is still a good judge and is satisfied because he dished out the consequence for the crime. How would you feel toward that person who took the sentence for you? What if the person who took the death sentence for you asked you to carry out his good mission? Would you do it?

The person who took that sentence for you and me is Jesus Christ the Son of the Living God! Even though we deserve the wrath of Almighty God, Jesus took the wrath for us. He came down as God in the flesh to redeem mankind from sin. He died on the cross for our sin.

But, Jesus just did not stay dead. The Scripture declares that on the third day God raised Jesus from the dead with all Power in His hand. Jesus pleased the God of the universe with His sacrifice. Not only did he resurrect Jesus, His return would forever allow those who believed in Jesus to have everlasting life in the kingdom of heaven with Him.

The Gospel of Jesus Christ is the most important Christian doctrine on earth. Without the Gospel we have nothing. The Gospel is the center of the universe and it should be studied, preached, and explained in every Christian work.

The Church is Beautiful

For a while now the church has been misunderstood. Some say they are tired of the churches' hypocritical actions. Heck, so am I. At the same time a lot of people do not know the purpose of the church. The church is not a building but it is the called out people of God, separated unto Him to accomplish His purpose.

Do you know why your church exists? Do you know why it is important to go to church? I am a firm believer that we, the Church, carry answers to the problems in this broken world. My pastor says, "We have no room to complain about ANYTHING if we are not bringing any solutions to the table." So, what do you dislike about church? Is what you dislike about church biblical? If so, please provide the scriptures for it.

What solutions are you bringing to the table that is in line with the Word of God? I encourage you to slow down and think about these questions and seek God for solutions according to the Word. Knowing fundamental doctrine (teaching) is so important and most of these teachings should be happening in the church. I love my church because it encourages me to take what I am being taught and check it with scripture. If a teaching/sermon does not line up with scripture then it will not be accepted.

Those who have issues with the church and refuse to attend should be able to define what the church is and know its purpose. God loves His Church and it is beautiful in His sight. Be careful how you talk about the Church of God. Jesus has purchased the Church with His own blood at Calvary and He is coming back for a Church without spot or blemish (Ephesians 5:27).

Some people who think they are a part of the Church may not be. The Scripture says, *He who says, "I know Him," and does not keep His commandments, is a liar, and the truth is not in him* (1 John 2:4).

Church
The Church is the hope of the world.
-Bill Hybels-

I want to talk about the purpose of church, the importance of the church and why you should not leave your church if you do not like some things about it.

What is the church? The church is the people of God. It is those who believe in the Gospel of Jesus and have accepted Him as Lord. The church is not the building you go to on Sundays. Yes, we call the building a church but in reality *you* are the church.

However, you cannot be the church by yourself. It is a group of believers who come together to worship, learn, serve and love one another. So, when we say I am about to go to church, we really should mean, "I am about to go worship God with other believers, help someone with their walk with God and to be encouraged in the faith through teaching, preaching and other believers."

The purpose of the local church is to equip you to do the work of the ministry. It is to help you find your purpose, gifts and passion then give you a platform to exercise your gifts through serving people. The church is the place where all your spiritual and life questions are to be answered according to scripture. It is the place where you are taught about who God is and how to live a life pleasing to Him. It is also the place to be connected with other believers and held accountable by your family in Christ. This is the place where we come to worship God together and stir up good works in one another.

The main function of the church is to reach the lost and meet the needs of the community. Ministry and good works should always result in salvation! Salvation and discipleship is the end goal of all Christian works. Jesus came to save all of mankind from the wrath of God. Young and older people are leaving the church in big numbers. Why? First, I believe that a lot of people do not know why they even go to church. I also believe that young people find church judgmental, boring and confusing.

This is where discipleship comes in. I want to challenge you to speak up in a biblical way concerning what you do not like about your church. The key word is biblical. I believe that you are the answer to the issues within your local church. In order to solve that issue, you must address it through the Bible. Be the change that you want to see. Do not leave just because you do not like it because we all need the church of God.

Yes, there may be a lot of traditions and things that you do not like about your church. As a Young Courageous Christian step up and bring solutions to the table to accomplish the purpose of the church. Please make sure it is biblical because the Bible is our direction to answer the problems you see within your church. Talk with your pastor and do not talk about him. Talk to your leaders and not about them. Ask the tough questions, pray, study and work at helping your church become as biblical as possible.

Unmask

Church is about loving, serving, encouraging and worshipping God with other believers. God has some gifts and good works in you and He uses His church to help you grow into your God potential. Remember the big goal is to save souls through the power of the Gospel of Jesus! Church is not designed to please your flesh and necessarily to have fun. It is about getting the Gospel out to the lost!

So, take off that church mask and stop going for show. Stop going to church to check it off your good-deeds-for-the-week list. Stop going just to hear a sermon and leaving without fulfilling the purpose God set up for the church. Change what you do as you are in church. Do not leave just because you do not like it. Do something about it in a biblical way.

Additional Scriptures to study:

Jerimiah 3:15, Matthew 16:13-19, Acts 2, 1 Corinthians 12:18,
Ephesians 4:11-16

Commitment:

_____
_____
_____
_____
_____
_____

Heaven
Heaven is all about the glory of Jesus Christ.
-Mo Brooks-

The White House is not important unless the President dwells there. A professional basketball, football or baseball game would not matter if the players did not show up. A school could not operate without an active principle. What I am trying to say is that we would not desire to go certain places if certain people were not there.

Heaven is not about NOT going to hell. It's about spending an eternity with Jesus. I heard a preacher ask this powerful question, "Would you want to go to heaven, with all its pleasures if Jesus was not there?" Be honest. Heaven is all about Jesus and us enjoying His presence forever. Heaven is about being free from sin, death, the flesh and worshipping our Lord forever.

Eternal life is a free gift from God Himself. There is evidence that you have received that free gift. That evidence is continual repentance of sin and doing the will of the Father. Heaven is all about King Jesus. So, do not get it twisted, there is no heaven without Jesus. Salvation through Jesus is the ticket to heaven and once you get there it is all about Jesus.

Unmask:

Desire heaven for Jesus, not because you do not want to go to hell. There is so much in the package of salvation and heaven is the ultimate prize. Jesus said in John 17:3, *And this is eternal life, that they may know You, the only true God, and Jesus Christ whom You have sent.* Heaven is all about Jesus!!!

Additional Scriptures to study:

John 3:16, 14:1-6, 17:3, Revelation 21 & 22 (chapters)

Commitment:

_____

_____

_____

_____

Hell
No one wants to go to Hell.
-Mo Brooks-

Hell is real and it was not made for humans. It was made for Satan and his servants. Hell is saved for those who have rejected the Gospel of Jesus Christ. God hates sin and has to punish all sin. Remember ,He is just. The punishment of sin against Him is hell, which is His wrath. Let us take a look at Matthew 25:31-46 but our focus will be on verse 41, *Then He will also say to those on the left hand, 'Depart from Me, you cursed, into the everlasting fire prepared for the devil and his angels.*

In these verses you find Jesus coming back and separating the saved from the unsaved. To the goats (or the unsaved group) Jesus says in verse 41, *Then He will also say to those on the left hand, Depart from Me, you cursed, into everlasting fire PREPARED FOR THE DEVIL AND HIS ANGELS."* See, God has no desire for anyone to go to hell. Hell is primarily for the devil and his angels.

In order to go to hell you have to flat out reject God! Please do not be deceived; going to church or merely confessing Jesus as Lord does not save you. Doing the will of the Father is what saves you from hell (Matthew 7:21). God's will is for you to believe in the Lord Jesus Christ and His Gospel. Belief in the Son of God, Jesus, is the great work we have to do (John 6:29). Since you believe in the Son of God you will pursue to please Him in every area of your life. When you sin (and you will sin) you will repent of sin and do not continue to walk in sin, lawlessness, transgressions or iniquity.

Unmask:

Use this section as motivation to be a witness and a Young Courageous Christian. Remember man does not have a heaven or hell to put another in. We are not the judge, God is. Our responsibility is to live an unmasked life and be courageous as we tell the world about Jesus. But first, we have to make sure our salvation is secure.

Additional Scriptures to study:

Matthew 7:21, 25:31-46, John 3:36, Romans 1:18, 2:5, Ephesians 5:6,
Read the Book of Revelation

Commitment:

_____

_____

_____

_____

_____

_____

Salvation (How do I know I am saved)
Make sure you are saved according to the requirements of scripture…
Know the evidence of your salvation.
-Mo Brooks-

This is a huge question, *how do I know I am saved?* We must answer this question according to Scripture. The answer seems simple: believe in the Lord Jesus. Believe that He lived, died, was resurrected and is coming back again. You must understand that merely saying that you believe is entirely different than really believing.

We say it all the time, but actions speak louder than words. That is so true when it comes to knowing that you are saved. Once you confess Jesus as Lord and believe unto salvation, there will be evidence of salvation. Once you receive salvation you are given a new heart through the regeneration of the Holy Spirit. This is your biggest evidence.

The Person of the Holy Spirit comes to dwell with you and cause you to hate sin as God does. And at the same time we are to love one another as God loves us. The Holy Spirit seals us until the day of redemption (Ephesians 1:13-14). God is in charge of this process not us. God does the saving and He does the sealing. God changes the heart and is the giver of the free gift of salvation.

I may be moving too fast so let me explain regeneration. We are all born with a sin nature/spirit that hates God and cannot help to disobey God (Psalm 51:5, Romans 3:23, Romans 5:12 and Ephesians 2:1-3). Once we truly believe in Jesus and are saved God regenerates our hearts and Spirit with His very own Spirit (Ezekiel 36:25-27, Romans 5:5, Titus 3:4-7).

Regenerations means, to be born again (John 3:3, 2 Corinthians 5:17). It means that the sin nature has been dealt away with and God has given the person a new Spirit that now has the capacity to love God (Ezekiel 11:18-20). All of this boils down to some key verses in Scripture that we have to pay attention to. You know you are save through keeping the Lords commandments. It is impossible to keep the commands of Jesus without the power of the Holy Spirit working through us (Read 1 John 2:4). This verse does not declare that we need to be perfect but it does declare that if we are walking in consistent sin without repentance we do not know God.

If we do not know God, we are not saved. Once you are truly born again/ saved no one can take that away from you (John 10:22-30). You cannot be unborn! You might ask, "Well what if a person was saved and then changed their mind about the faith?" I will say, they never believed in the first place (Hebrews 6:4-6).

How do you know you are saved? By confessing sin, growing in repentance of sin, keeping the commandments of God and being a witness. As you study the Scripture you will see the clear line that is drawn in the sand between the believer and unbeliever. It is really not that hard to see. Just be careful because there is a lot of teaching out there that says you can be saved and live any type of way. That is so false and far from the Truth.

Unmask

I believe I am saved 100%, but that does not stop me from checking my salvation. I still look at what the believer should be doing through Scripture and I continue to repent when I fall short of the standard of God. I encourage you to do the same. Do you really love God? Have you really believed unto salvation?

If you have doubts about your salvation, I encourage you to go before God in prayer surrendering to Him. Give all to our Lord Jesus. Speak with a leader at your church to walk with you through Scriptures explaining more about your salvation. Do not walk around with the mask of Christianity on without salvation.

Additional Scriptures to study:

Genesis 3:15, Isaiah 53:1-12, Ezekiel 36:25-29, Matthew 7:21-29, John 3:16, 10:25-30, Romans 5:6-11, 10:9-13, 2 Corinthians 5:12-21, Ephesians 2:4-9

Commitment:

_____

_____

_____

Praise
Let everything that has breathe Praise the Lord.
Psalm 150:6

It does not matter how much we thank God, it will always fall short of just how much He does for us. Due to the mercies and goodness of God we ought to praise Him all the time. The definition of praise is simply giving verbal thanks to God for what He has done and who He is. Churches get together and praise differently. The important thing is that our praise is biblical.

Look and see how God wants to be praised. Since He demands praise from His people, we ought to seek Him to see how He wants us to praise. There are a lot of churches that do a lot of shouting, dancing and so forth. That is okay. If you are not accustomed to that then find a place of worship where you can praise God without putting on any masks. There are a lot of churches and I believe God is saying that there is no excuse not to be a part of one.

There is only one requirement for praise and that is to be breathing. Psalm 150:6 says, *Let everything that has breath praise the Lord. Praise the Lord!* Think about it, you do not have to have a relationship with someone to say thank you. I say thank you to strangers all the time when I see fit. If you are alive it is because of God and that deserves a thank You every day.

Unmask

You should not have to put on a mask just to praise God. You should be able to praise Him according to Scripture. Read these scriptures and see when, where, why and how God wants us to praise Him. Then praise Him at home in secret and at church! There is so many other scriptures on praise, I just choose a few.

Additional Scriptures to study:

Psalm 103, 105, 107, 111, 122, 136, 145-150, Hebrews 13:15,
1 Peter 2:9-10

Commitment:

_____

_____

_____

Worship
Worship Daily.
-Mo Brooks-

Worship is a lifestyle. It takes place every day. God will reject our worship if it is not done properly. If Sunday is the only time you worship then you did not worship. We worship God for who He is. Knowing the attributes of God is so important because it is difficult to worship God without knowing who He is.

I love reading the story of Moses because I find almighty God teaching Moses who He is and how to worship. Worship includes prayer, praise, obedience to His Word, meditation and a heart to please God.

Remember this is a lifestyle that is why it is so important to have discipline to carryout worship every day. We cannot get distracted so much that we do not worship. Worship does not happen automatically but it is purposefully and meaningful.

Unmask

Do you live a lifestyle of worship? Worship begins at home! Begin worshipping God by yourself at home and watch it carryover throughout your entire day. Worship is birthed out of spending that quality time with God. Worship according to the scripture and repent from sin that God may accept your worship.

Additional Scriptures to study:

Psalm 96:6, Isaiah 6:1-9, Matthew 28:17, John 4:4-26, Romans 12:1-2
*Moses and Abraham is great examples of worshippers

Commitment:

_____
_____
_____
_____
_____
_____
_____

Giving
The most selfish act to do is to give.
-Denzel Washington-

There is no greater joy in the world than to give away something to benefit another. That is why Denzel Washington said, "The most selfish act to do is to give," because when you give, with the right motives, you experience pure joy. Giving is biblical and should be practiced among believers. Many people question giving in the church and do not trust it.

When we give of ourselves and money, we are acting just like God. For God is a giver and every good and perfect gift comes from Him. The money you have is not yours; it belongs to God. If it were not for God nothing would exist. He is Lord over all. God is the director of our giving and but we have to allow Him to. God only asks us to give 10% of your first fruits (earnings).

As we mature in Christ He may ask you to give more or give to a mission group. If God demands us to give then He has to provide for us to give. We are blessed to be a blessing. Do not be selfish with the gifts of God but bless the ministry that you benefit from. For in blessing the ministry of God, ministry goes forth and lives are saved.

Unmask:

God wants you to see your own heart through giving. He knows all things. When you give to your local church you are giving to save and change lives. It takes money to do ministry and the end goal of any ministry is to save souls. Start giving your 10% and manage the rest with godly fear.

Additional Scriptures to study:

Malachi 3:8-12, Matthew 6:19-21, John 3:16, 2 Corinthians 8:1-15,
Philippians 4:19

Commitment:

_____
_____
_____
_____
_____

Baptism
There is nothing special or holy about the water in the baptism pool.
-Mo Brooks-

Baptism does not save you but it is an outward expression of what has taken place on the inside. Baptism shows how we identify with Christ. When we believed and obeyed the Gospel we also die to self.

When we are baptized we show our commitment outwardly. There is nothing special about the water we are baptized in. However it symbolizes that we believe in Christ and that he died and rose on the third day. Our symbolic burial tells the world that our sins are forgiven.

Baptism is a commandment from God. Even Jesus was baptized. I truly believe that Jesus would not tell us to do anything that He would not do for the Lord. Baptism is a time of celebrating another sibling being added to the body of Christ.

Unmask:

Celebrate baptism in your church because it is declaring that another soul has been added to His kingdom. Remember baptism does not save you or wash away sin. Only the blood of Jesus can do that!

Additional Scriptures to study:

Matthew 3:13-17, 28:19, Romans 6:1-7

Commitment:

_____

_____

_____

_____

_____

_____

_____

Communion
The third Monday in January is always MLK Day
-Fact-

Why is there a Martin Luther King Jr. day? To answer that question we must ask, what did he do to lead to such an honor? King stood up and spoke out for equality during the Civil Rights movement. He went to jail and in the end was killed for what he believed in.

The King holiday is a way to remember and honor his works. The way you honor someone is to remember their mission and carry it out once they are gone. Well that is what communion is all about.

Communion is all about remembering Jesus and what He did for us on the cross. Only a believer should take part of this because unbelievers do not have anything to remember concerning the salvation of their souls. Communion cannot be taken for the forgiveness of sin. The main function is to remember Jesus (Matthew 26 and 1 Corinthians 11). For those who do not know, Communion takes place when the church eats a piece of bread (symbolizing Jesus' body) and drinks a small cup of grape juice (symbolizing his blood that was spilled on the cross) to remember Jesus' sacrifice.

Unmask:

You must be a believer in order to take communion and while you take communion your mind must be on Jesus. This is not a time to repent or receive salvation but to simple remember the death, burial and resurrection of our Lord and Savior Jesus.

Additional Scriptures to study:

Matthew 26 and 1 Corinthians 11

Commitment:

_____
_____
_____
_____
_____

Hypocrite
Let your yes be yes and your no be no.
-Jesus-

I put "hypocrite" in this section instead of the temptation section due to the term being commonly used in conjunction with the church. People say that the church is full of hypocrites. I define the term hypocrite as a person who says they are one thing but actions are completely the opposite.

Jesus described the Pharisees and Scribes as hypocrites in his day. They said they loved God and follow the law of God but in reality they were doing the exact opposite. The Pharisees and Scribes wore a mask of Christianity or in that day Judaism. No one likes a hypocrite because it means that they are fake, liars and out to deceive others.

This is the hypocrite test question: Does the person do what they claim to do with the motive they say they are doing it for? Now, it is hard to speak about someone's motives; only God sees all of that. So, is the church full of hypocrites? I would say no, but I have not been to every church.

There may be hypocrites in the church and that is expected. The church is a hospital where "sick" people go to get help. Just because there are a few people who are perceived to be hypocrites, that should not stop you from getting what you need through the church.

I am sure that there are hypocrites at the grocery store, library, parties, clubs, and just about any place that you go. Hypocrites do not stop you from going to these places. So, why use that excuse that the church has hypocrites not to go? No one should stop you from receiving what God has for you.

Jesus died for the hypocrite, liar and deceiver. When I find myself being hypocritical, I repent. Before you deem everyone in church "a bunch of hypocrites" check yourself. Treat others as you want to be treated. You never know, you might be the believer that encourages that hypocrite walk straight before God and man.

Unmask:

Check yourself before calling others hypocrites (Matthew 7:3-5). Be the change you want to see. Build relationships, encourage and help people whose words and actions contradict themselves. Do not give up on church because the faults of others may have been exposed. Do not allow someone else's sin against God—or even perceived sin—hinder your walk with Jesus. Make sure your word and your actions line up. Be who you say you are!

Additional Scriptures to study:

Matthew 23, Romans 2:17-24, James 3:1

Commitment:

_____

_____

_____

_____

Bible Stories

Sometimes popular Bible characters like Noah, David, Paul and many others are looked at as types of superheroes. In reality the people in the Bible are regular human beings like you and I. God used them in a mighty way and he can use you as well.

Do not be afraid to learn about these people, their successes and failures. Read their stories, study their habits and find out the good, bad and ugly about their lives. For we can learn a lot about God and ourselves as we look at these people.

Unmask

Read and study the "popular" people and stories of the Bible. They will bless your life because you will pick up some great nuggets and habits to build your life on.

Additional Scriptures to study:

Look up the stories like the Flood, Red Sea, Jericho wall, David and Goliath. Read them, learn from them and apply godly principles to your life!

Commitment:

_____

_____

_____

_____

1 John: The Test

I had to single out this particular book of the Bible because I believe it is the litmus test of the Christian. If you want to know if you are in the faith, just read this book. If you want to know the requirements of the Christian, just read this book. This book in the Bible will challenge you on your Christianity like no other. It is direct and straight to the point. Being a Young Courageous Christian can be difficult at time but it sure is worth it because God is always on your side.

Unmask

Read 1 John and see how you line up with Scripture. Make the necessary adjustments to line up with your faith. Repent in the areas you need to repent.

Additional Scriptures to study:
1 John

Commitment:

_____
_____
_____
_____
_____
_____
_____
_____

Additional
UNMASKing
Tools

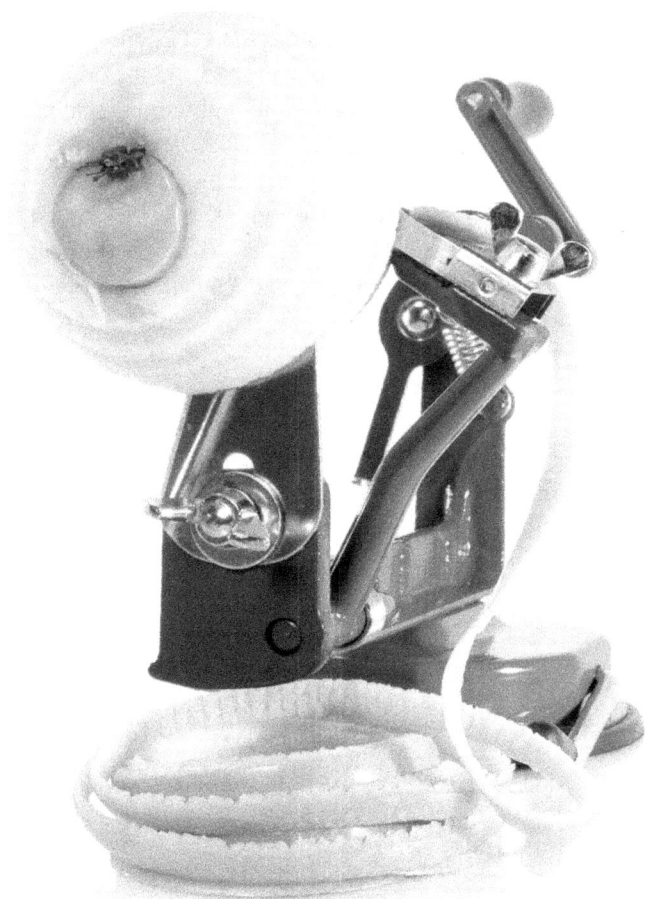

Great Bible Tools to Read

There are some great tools out there to help you understand and dig deeper in you Bible. The best tool is your obedience to the Scriptures though. When you obey the Word, you will understand the Word more deeply.

Here is a short list of Bible tools:

Purchase, borrow or check out from the library any *Exhaustive Concordance of the Bible*. In this you will find every word in the Bible in this Concordance. Not only will you find every word you may want the definition to, you will find the proper meanings. Remember the Bible was not originally written in English, so biblical words have different meanings than our English language.

If you cannot afford an exhaustive concordance of the Bible visit the website www.blueletterbible.org.

Systematic Theology by Grudem

This book is awesome when it comes to the attributes of God. This book is huge and has a lot of information in it about who God is, who we are and all major subjects of Christianity.

Bible Dictionary

A Bible dictionary is just great to have to explain biblical terms. There are many to choose from so I recommend you find the one that best suits you.

The History of the Bible

This book has a lot of pictures and really shows how the Bible came to be. It has a lot of good information on the Word of God. Check it out and ignore any pictures of Jesus as no one has ever had an accurate picture of him based on his description in the Bible.

The New How to Study Your Bible

This book really shows you practical ways to study your Bible. It teaches you how to see common threads and key words as well.

Authors I Enjoy

I love reading books from "old-school" preachers. I enjoy being challenge by the Scriptures to live a holy, prayerful and pleasing life to God. Here are some authors that I take pleasure in reading and listening too:

Pastor Addis Moore

Charles H. Spurgeon

Leonard Ravenhill

Andrew Murray

C.S. Lewis

Ravi Zacharias

Christian Music

Music is a huge influence on our society today. I believe that in every song (with spoken words) there is a sermon being preached. Every song has a message that the artist is trying to communicate to their audience. There is Christian rock, jazz, rap and just about another genre you can think of. It is easy to find and test out Christian music for yourself. Just Google/Youtube/Pandora Christian Rap music and you will find a lot of music you can listen to. Contact me, @mo_brooks if you have any trouble finding Christian music.

Daily Reading Challenge

How often do you read your Bible? Be honest and remember we are unmasking and keeping it real. I told you this in chapter one but let me give you a little more detail. When I first started walking with Christ I made two commitments to Him. Those two commitments were to go to church every Sunday and to read at least one chapter of my Bible every day.

I thought that these were great commitments because I was not doing either one of them at all. So, my logic told me that God would be pleased if I read at least one chapter a day. To this day I think He is pleased with my commitment. This commitment changed my entire life!

When I first began my commitment I heard God speak to me for the first time. Most importantly I began to know the heart of God and what He wanted from me. It is impossible to live the Christina life, especially young and courageously, without studying and applying what you study. The purpose of this challenge is not for you to remember Scripture but to know the heart of God that you may obey His will for your life. So, I want to challenge you right now.

I challenge you to read one chapter of your Bible every day. I do not want you to put it on social media and share it with the world. I want you to just spend time with God every day. The entire chapter two of this book is dedicated to giving you great places to start so you do not have that excuse, "where do I start?"

If you read three chapters of the Bible in one day that does not mean you get to take a two days off. Read your one chapter the next day. This challenge will change your life forever. Your prayer life will increase as a result of this challenge.

You can do it. I am here to help you in any way possible! Contact me through email, mobrooksycc@gmail.com; Twitter @mo_brooks or Facebook "Morris Mo Brooks" if you have any questions or need help.

Social Media Challenge

Millions of people are logged into some form of social media network every day and receiving all types of messages, posts, updates and tweets. As a Young Courageous Christian, what are you posting? Posting things about your life and events is okay. Remember that the Christians carry the responsibility of being a witness.

There are people who read your posts and tweets that need you. They need your positive godly messages every day. They need your encouragement and challenge to be who they say they are. They need to see your post and tweets line up with the faith you claim.

So, if you do not post/tweet godly things, who will? I am talking about that will reach the unsaved people that you know. What impact for Christ are you having through your social media account? Again I am not telling you not to post what is going on in your life and events. I am encouraging you to watch the evil things that you post and to increase the godly posts. Make sure that your social media accounts line up with who you say you are.

I found this out to be true among many young people. If you are ashamed or afraid to post about Jesus and Scripture on a regular bases then you are probably not living a life pleasing to Him. It is hard to post godly things on Facebook and tweet about Jesus on Twitter when you are not being who you say you are consistently—at least that is true in my life.

Your Challenge

I challenge you to grow by accepting two challenges.

#1- Post/Tweet one Godly scripture post every day for 31 days straight using #YCC1 (the 1 is for day 1). During this time you are not to post anything ungodly or foolish!

#2- After the 31 days are up, only post things on social media that will benefit someone else in a Godly way. Life events and personal things are okay, but remember people are following you and are impacted by what you post. So, use social media as an outlet to serve and help other people.

Ready for the challenge? Make sure you follow me on Twitter @mo_brooks and friend me on Facebook at "Morris Mo Brooks". I am here to help you and encourage you in any type of way!

Test Answers

Below are the answers to the pre-test in the beginning of the book:

God is **_perfect_** because He never has or will make a mistake, wrong decision or sin.

God is **_holy_** because He is like no other. He is set apart from everything and everyone.

God is **_all-powerful_** because He has unlimited power.

God is **_all-present_** because He is everywhere at the same time.

God is **_all-knowing_** because He knows all things (past, present and future; nothing is hidden from Him).

God is **_faithful_** because He will always and forever keep His promises! God is loyal and He cannot lie.

God is the **_creator_** because all things are made by Him.

God is the **_sustainer_** because He is the One who holds all things in place e.g. the earth rotation, planets orbit and water separated from the land.

God is **_just_** because He is fair and all of His decisions are righteous.

God is **_merciful_** because He gives sinners time to repent.

God is **_gracious_** because He blesses sinners when they do not deserve it.

God is **_love_** for He died for the entire world that they may be saved.

God is **_wrathful_** because He will punish and judge all sin.

God is **_jealous_** because He despises anything receiving worship besides Himself.

God is **_eternal (self-existing)_** because no one created Him. God always existed. He is the beginning and the end.

About the Author

Morris "Mo" Brooks is a native of West Michigan who has a passion to see Christ's character in the lives of his generation and beyond. He serves as an associate minister at Mt. Zion Baptist Church in Kalamazoo, Michigan under the leadership of the Rev. Dr. Addis Moore.

Mo holds a Bachelors of Art Degree in social psychology from Western Michigan University. This is his debut book.

For more information or questions,
visit <u>www.mobrooks1.com</u>

www.ingramcontent.com/pod-product-compliance
Lightning Source LLC
LaVergne TN
LVHW021515080426
835509LV00018B/2520